Coloring Book of Animals and Birds for Kids

Riya Sharma

Copyright © All rights reserved
Disclaimer

All Rights Reserved. No part of this book may be reproduced in any form without permission in writing from the author.

While all attempts have been made to verify the information provided in this publication, neither the author nor the publisher assumes any responsibility for errors, omissions, or contrary interpretations of the subject matter herein.

This book is for entertainment purposes only. The views expressed are those of the author alone, & should not be taken as expert instruction or commands. The reader is responsible for his or her own actions. Adherence to all applicable laws & regulations, including international, federal, state laws governing professional licensing, business practices, advertising & all other aspects of business, or any other jurisdiction is the sole responsibility of the purchaser or reader.

Neither the author nor the publisher assumes any responsibility or liability whatsoever on the behalf of the purchaser or reader of these materials. Any perceived slight of any individual or organization is purely unintentional.

Preamble

Coloring is a great exercise for the brain, stimulating both hemispheres and fostering the development of creativity, visual perception, abstract thinking, and emotional intelligence. This activity makes children think about themselves, their environment and helps them understand the world better. This is why many children draw pictures of themselves and their family and friends.

The instinct that children have for painting is incredible. From a very young age, we can give them a pencil and a sheet that they start scribbling on their own. For them, it is a way of communicating, of expressing emotions and feelings that perhaps they have not yet verbalized. And, in addition to being a very fun activity, the benefits of coloring pages are numerous, both for children and adults.

While coloring, the child is not aware of anything else, his only goal is to do his best and therefore ignores other distractions. In addition, it also enhances self-control and helps you channel emotions. It is a perfect activity for you to spend time with yourself, disconnect from everything else, and relax your mind.

Another benefit of coloring pages is that it is an activity that can be done both alone and in a group, and it is also not necessary to have great skills. This makes it a joyful and very satisfying activity, helping to improve your self-esteem. And, on top of that, if they are later congratulated for their work, all the better!

Coloring is an activity that we always associate with children. Most of us remember it as a fun endeavor where you could be as creative as possible, using all the available colors. But as we get older, we decide that we are too old to continue coloring and that the only adults who should do this kind of thing are graphic artists.

The action of coloring needs our brain to enter a state of creativity to be able to mix and match colors, but it must also apply logic to be able to understand what figures are being formed when coloring. For the brain to do all this it needs to activate the cerebral cortex which is where sight and motor skills are managed, necessary to make small and precise movements when coloring. The whole process means that we have to concentrate on a single activity that is fun and that, in addition, reminds us of good moments of our childhood, which, in turn, makes us put aside the worries of adult life and the stress, even for a few minutes a day.

Sleep is an important part of life, but unfortunately, many people suffer from insomnia. There are many remedies for this problem, but there are also therapies to help you sleep regularly. One of them is color therapy, which is based on how color stimulates us. For example, blue and white are colors that have a relaxing effect on the nervous system, while red raises blood pressure and pulse.

This is when color therapy goes a bit further. The activity would relax your mind to the point of eliminating the anxiety you felt every time you had to go to sleep. This happens because the use of colors and the concentration required for the task force the brain to live in the moment, without elements of competition or possible failure.

Some people find drawing and coloring relaxing, we can spend so much time focusing on the details that each drawing, and fragment, is satisfying. Not long ago focused coloring books for adults became popular, it seems that we are growing and if we do not dedicate ourselves to the fine arts we can forget the tranquility that drawing provides.

According to Buddhism, coloring pictures not only provides relaxation but also each color and shape has a purpose for physical, psychic, and spiritual healing. Similarly likewise with meditation.

Experts have studied the relationship between coloring and reducing anxiety, and some of the studies prove that the activity produces a sense of calm similar to what we feel when we meditate deeply or do a pleasant activity.

The books offer a variety of bird illustrations. When coloring you can forget about the problems and 'disconnect from the noise' of the worries that cause us anxiety. Also, you can forget about the rules; although the ideal is to paint between the lines, there are no limits; you can do it your way. You have complete freedom to select the colors and the time you spend coloring will depend only on you.

Among other advantages of this activity is being able to realize how your mood changes every day. You will find out when selecting the color palette. Coloring will allow you to enjoy making simple decisions and practicing patience.

This activity not only allows you to remember childhood but also helps reduce stress levels. It also promotes concentration, revives aspects of creativity, and keeps the practitioner busy for a long time, thus avoiding the prolonged use of electronic devices and social networks.

Why not try this new form of entertainment? You can do this activity in the company of your grandchildren or create a club or group to color with your friends. You can try this during times of great anxiety, such as when you are about to get on a plane or during a flight. Some people report that doing this activity before going to sleep helps them prepare for a good night's rest.

Remember, the only rules when coloring is to let go and enjoy the moment. Now, let start coloring…

—**Author**

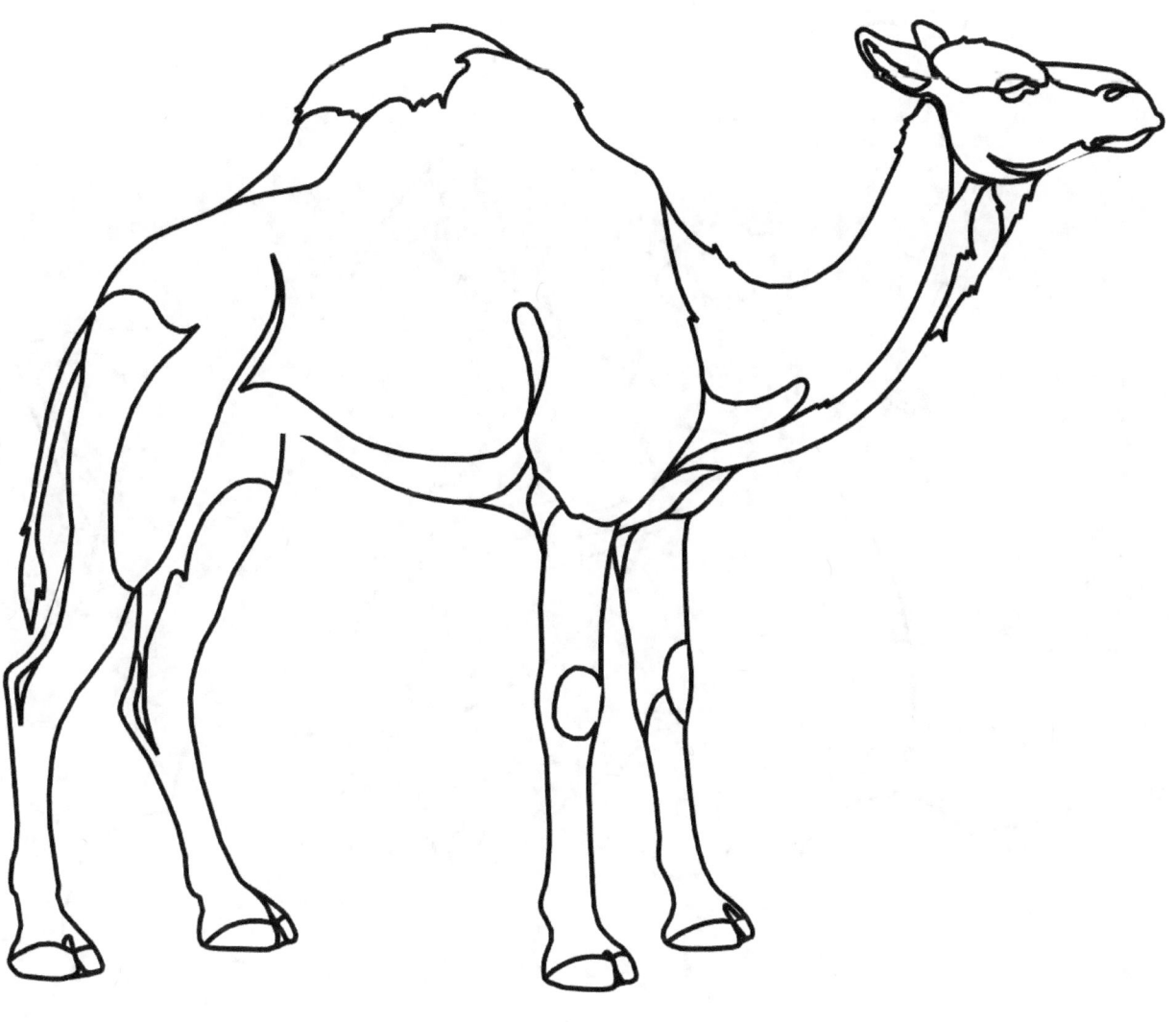

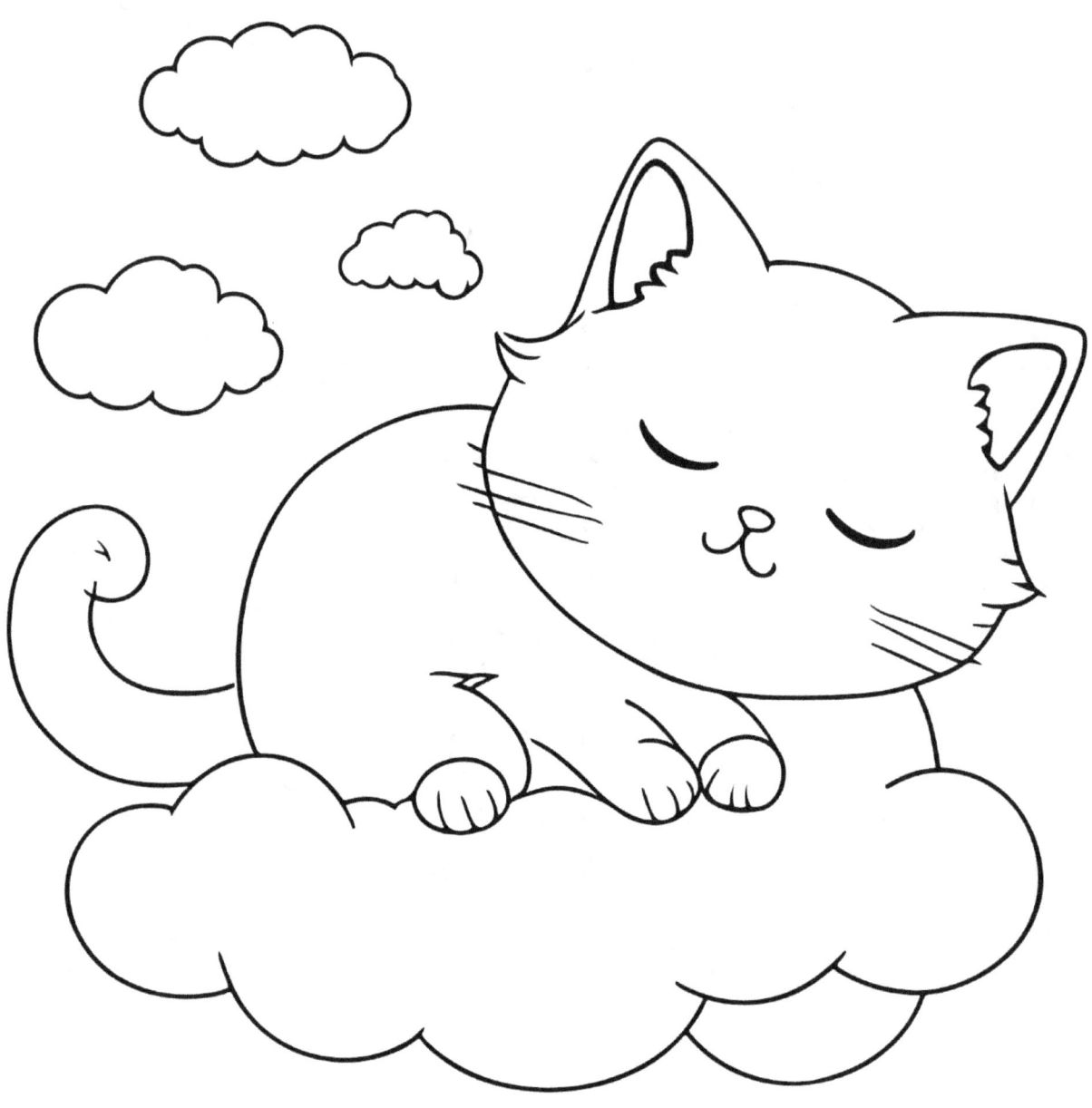

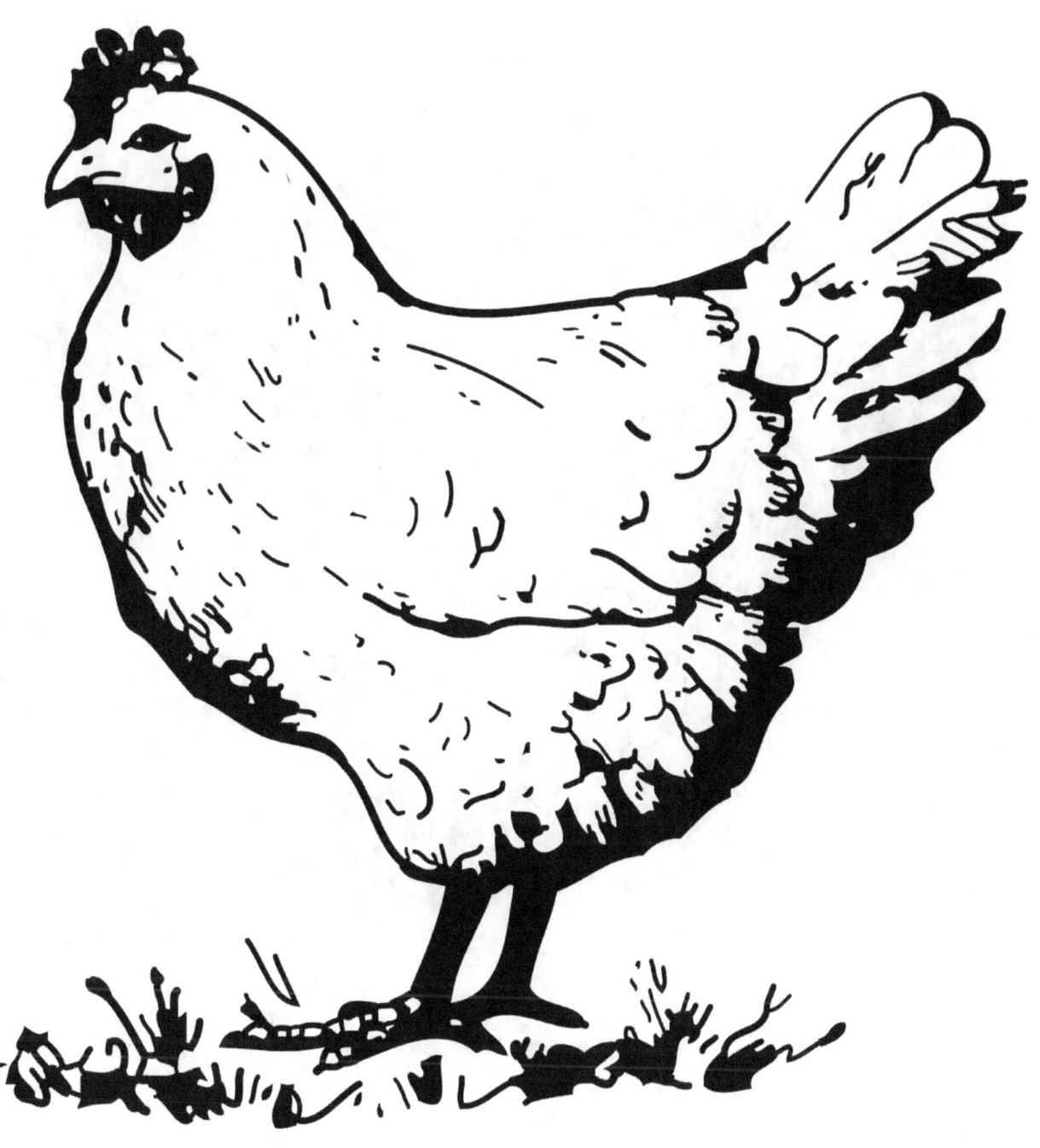

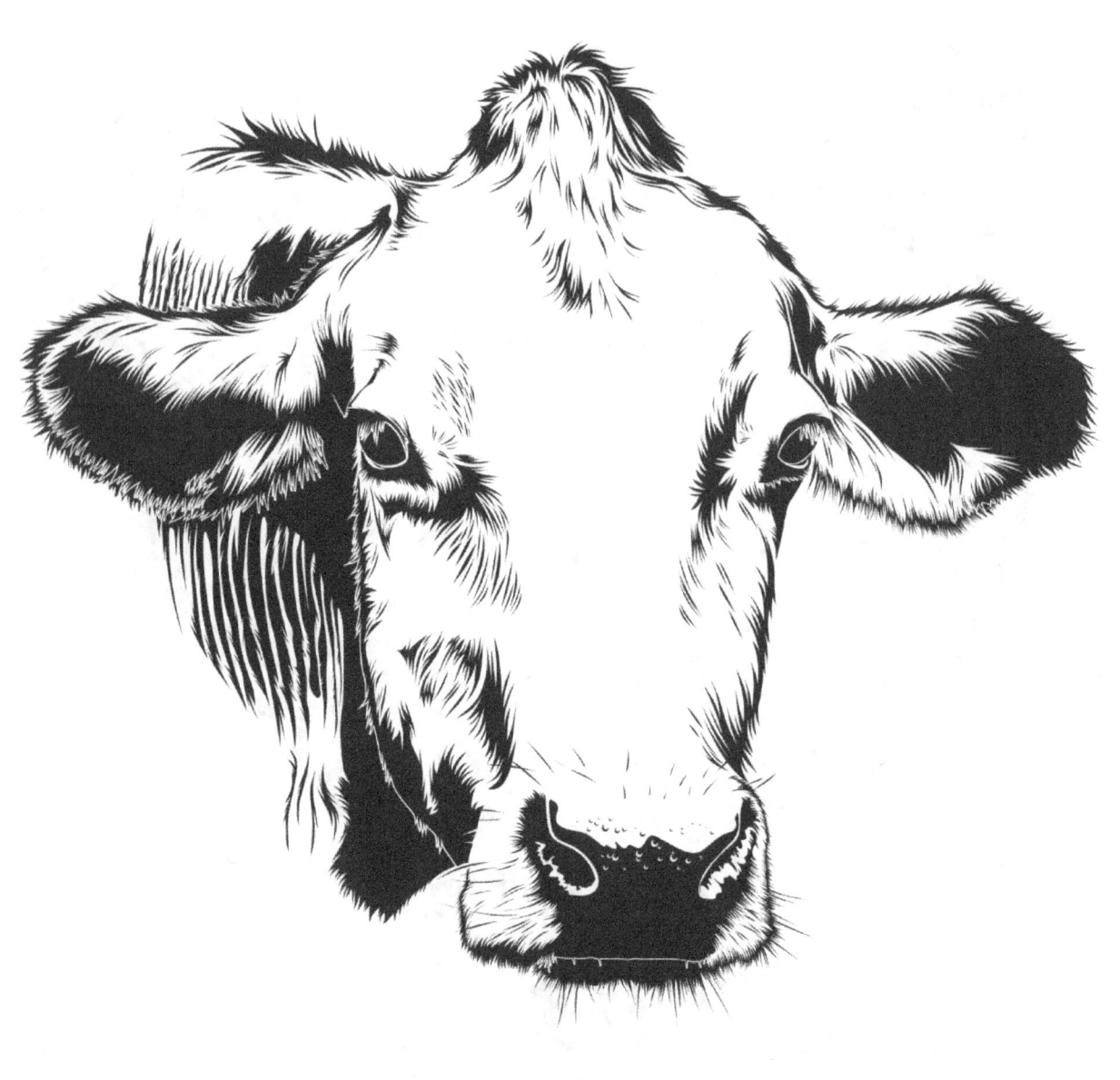

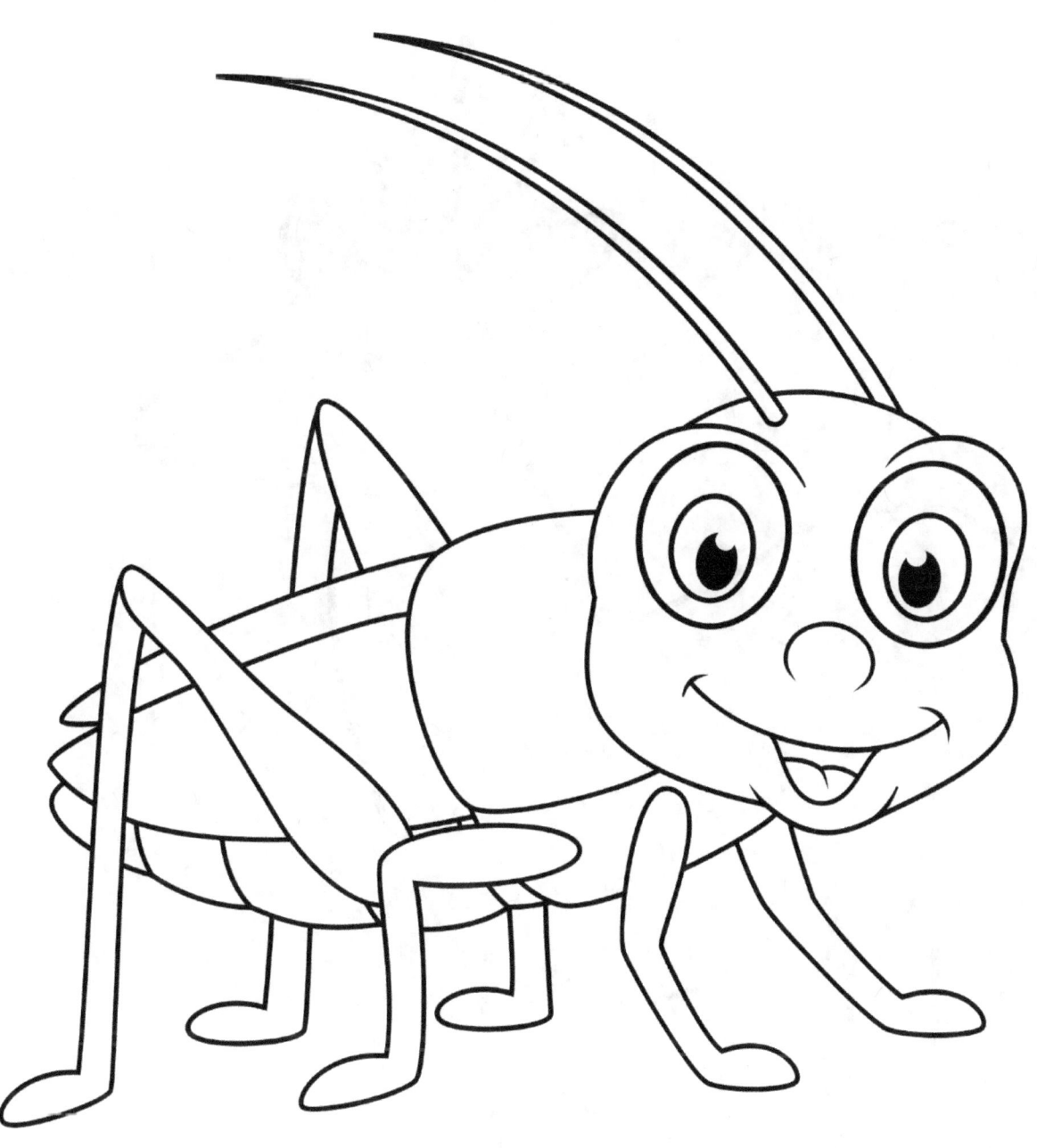

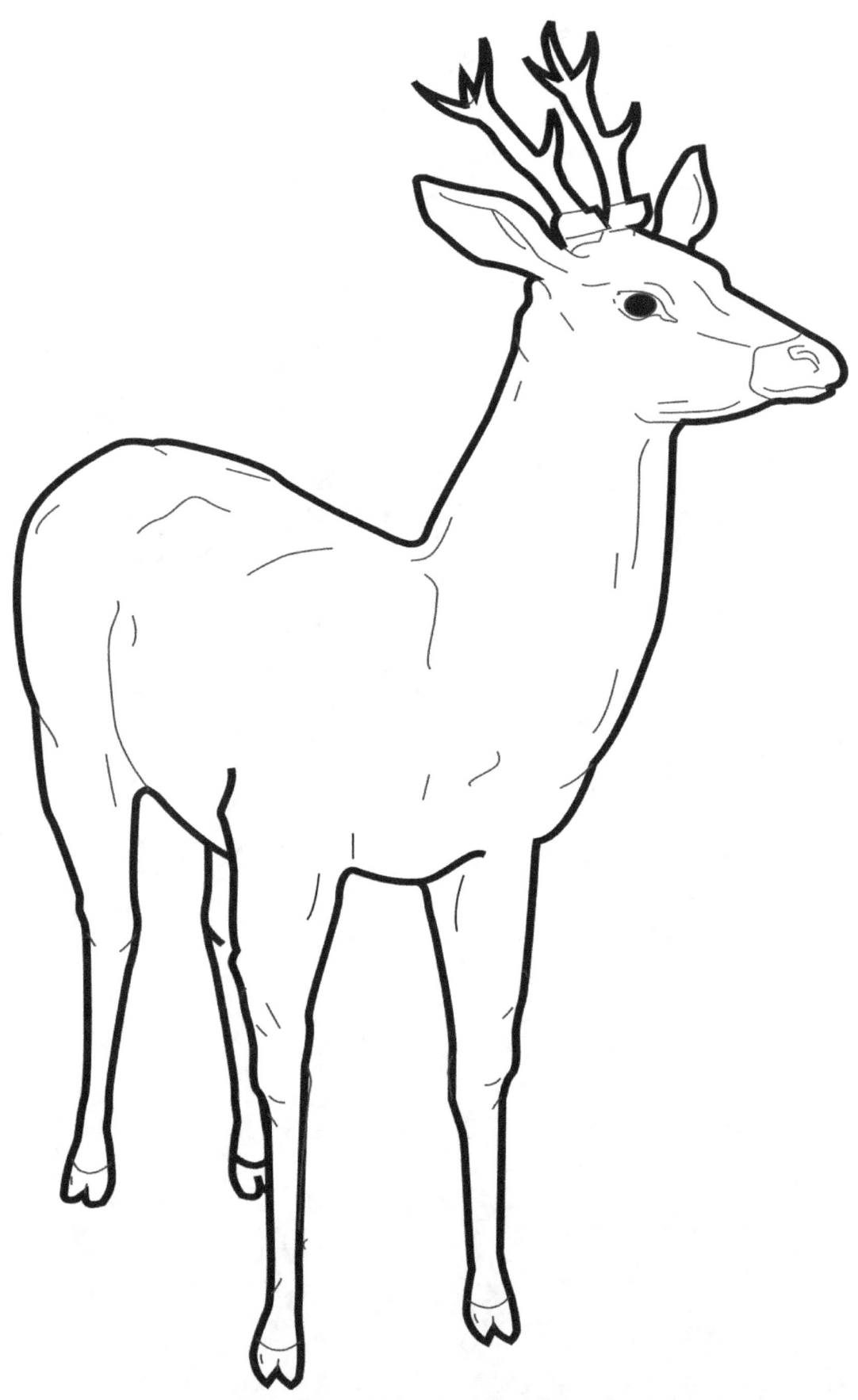

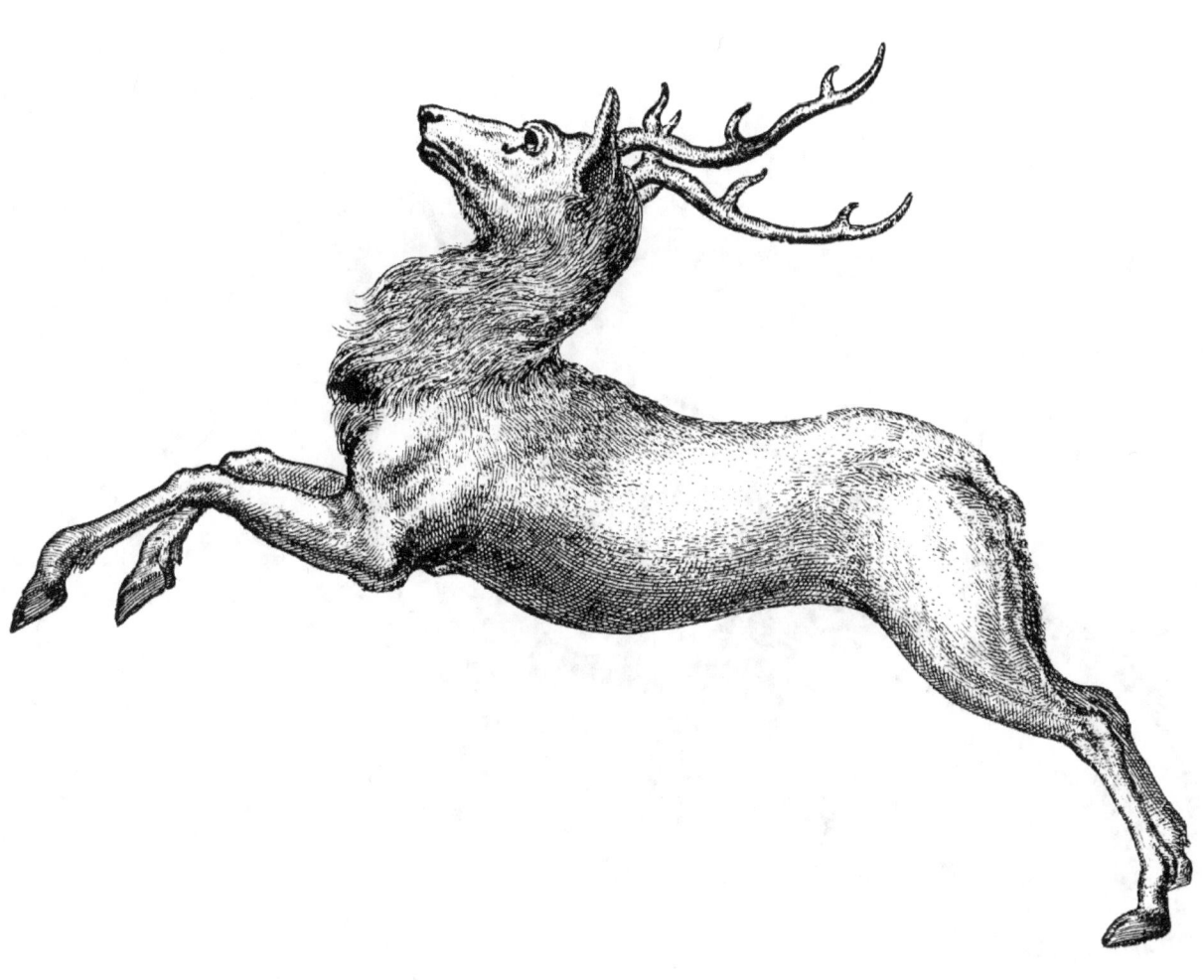

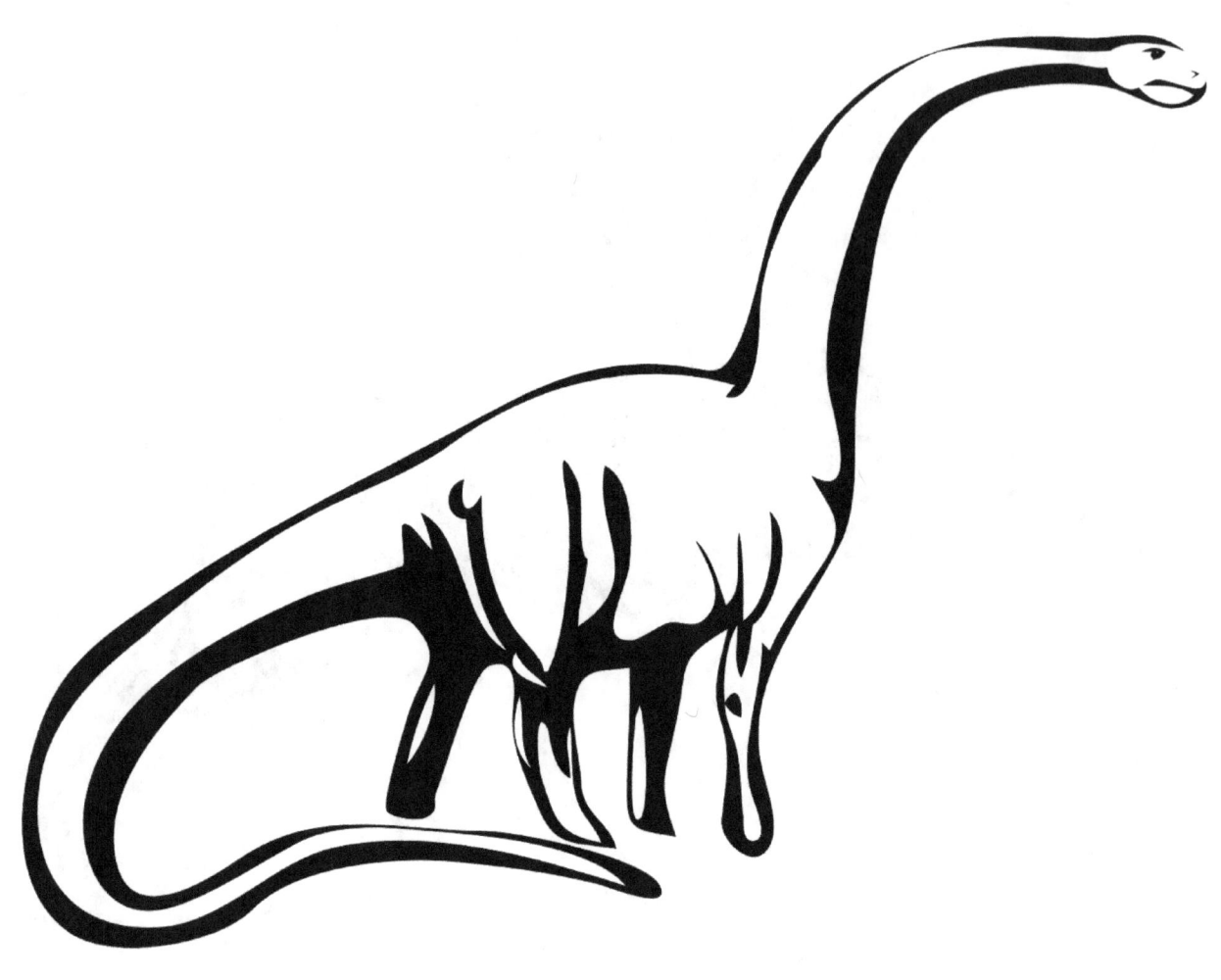

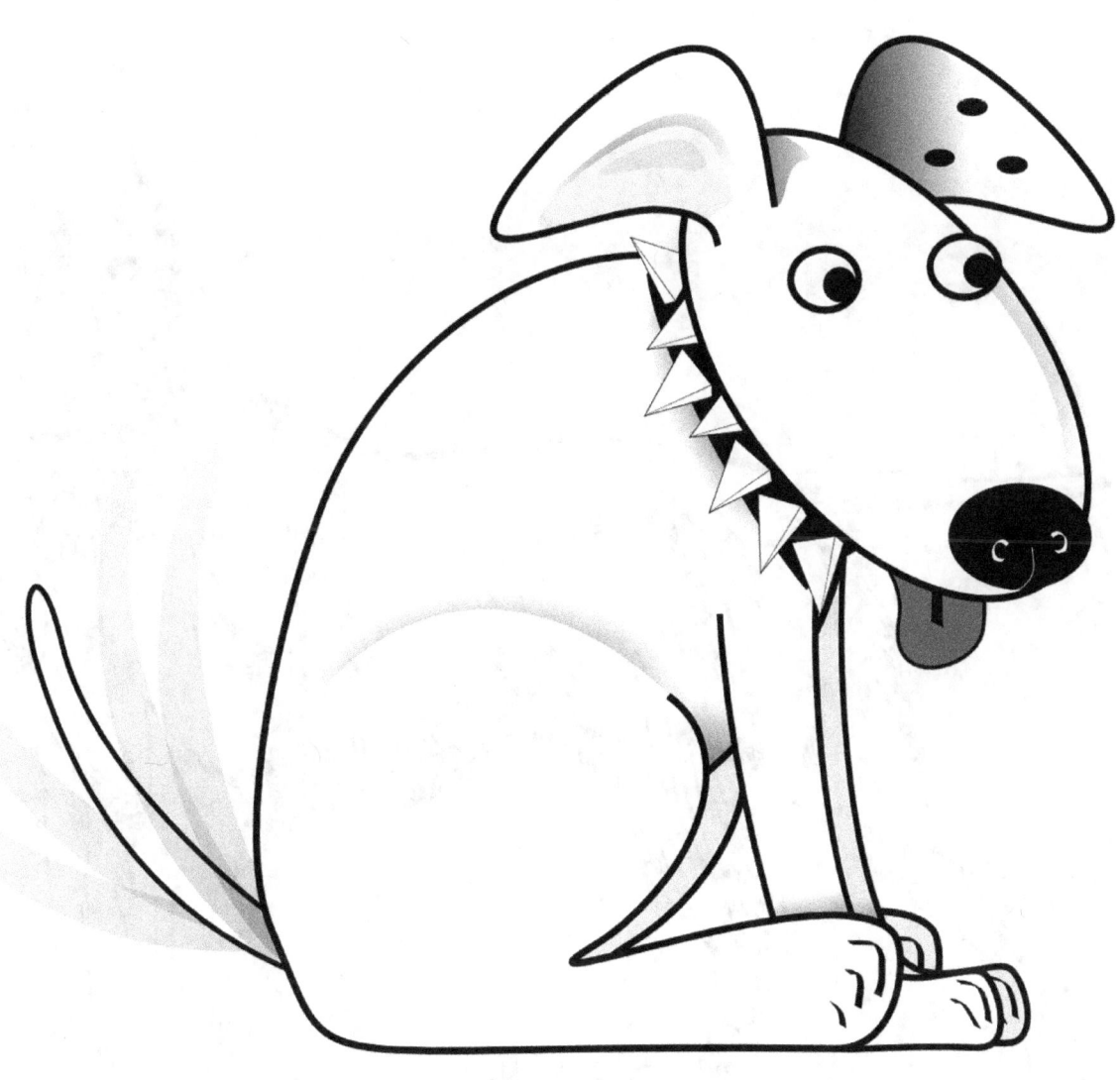

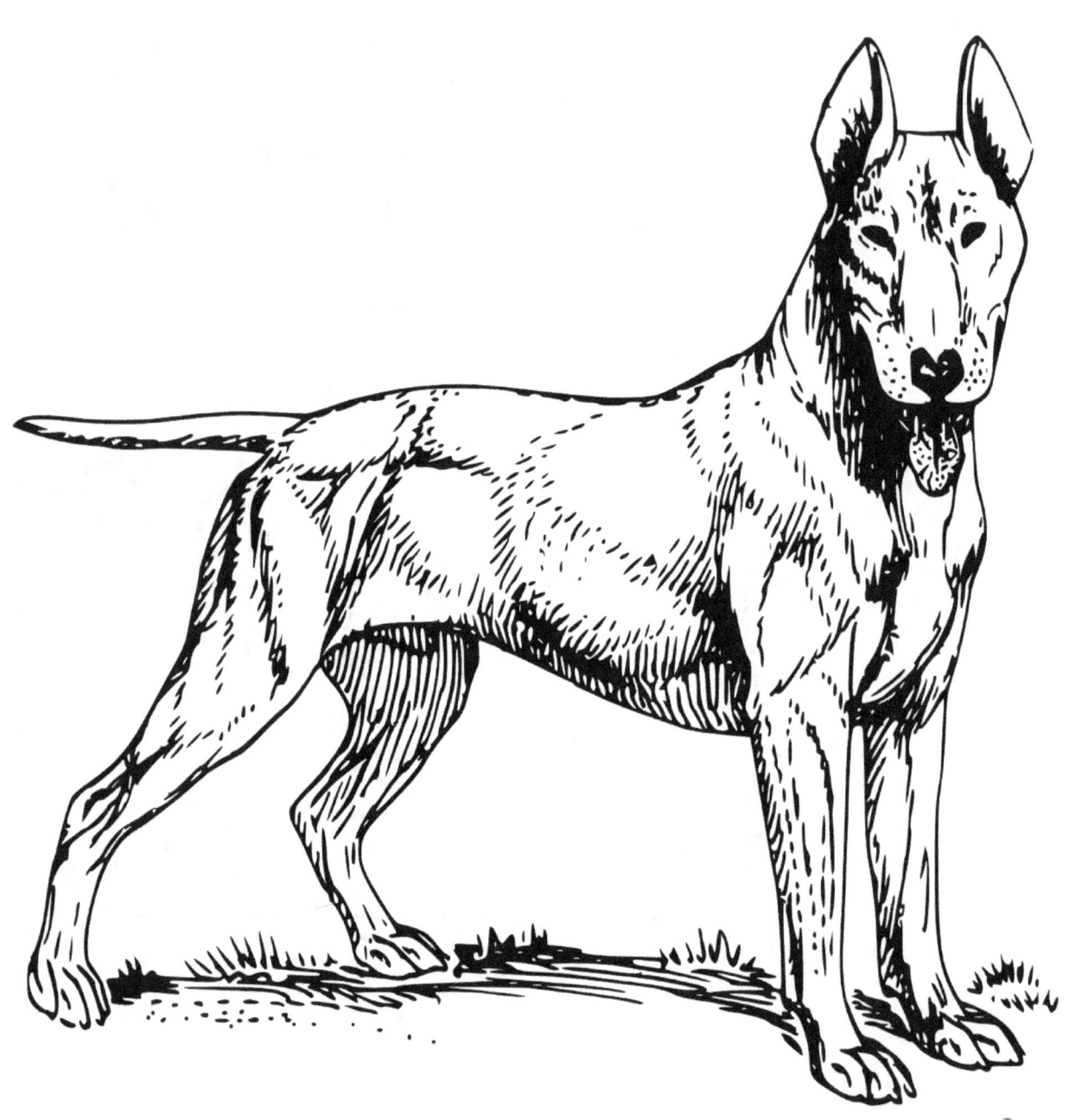

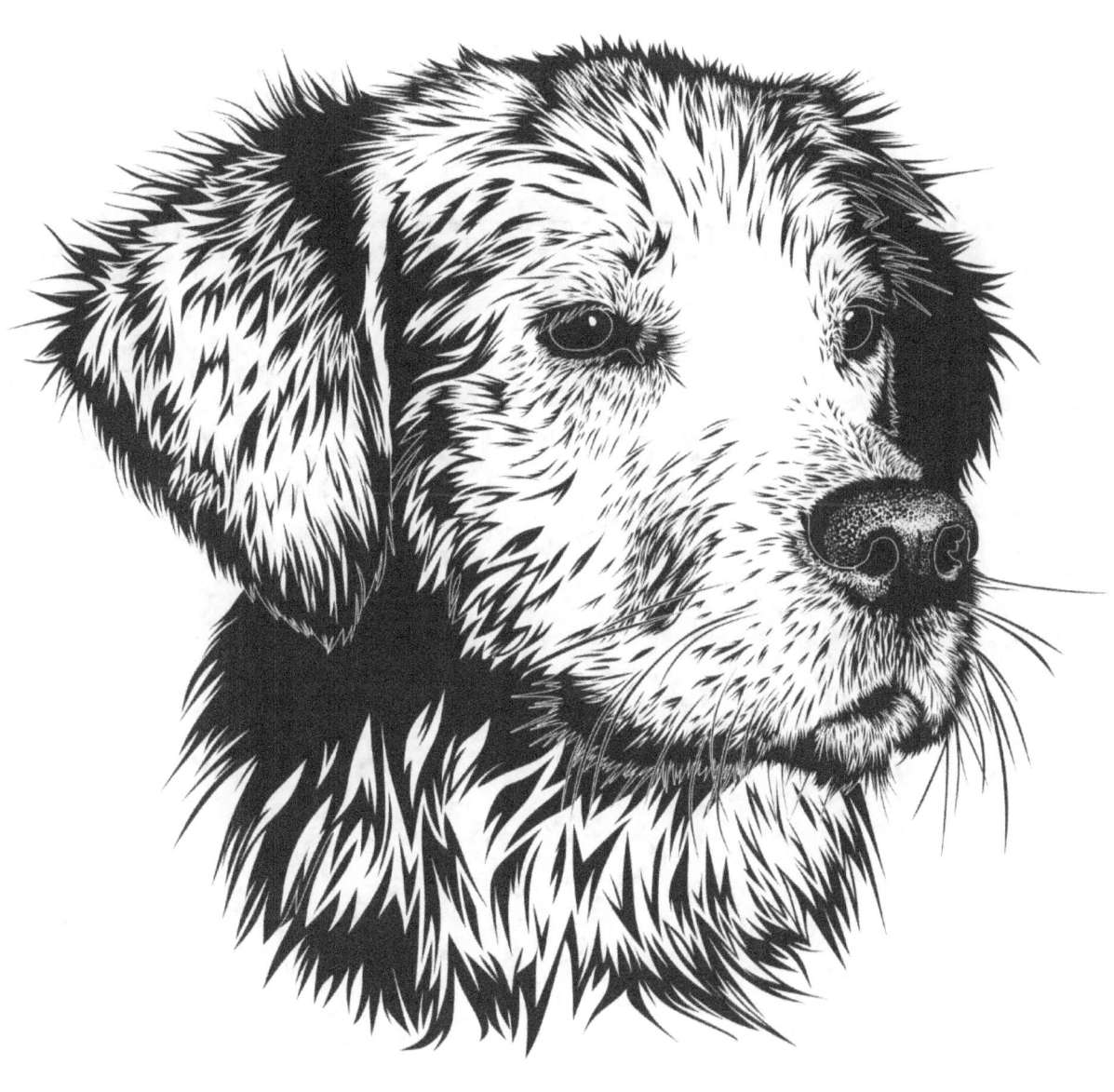

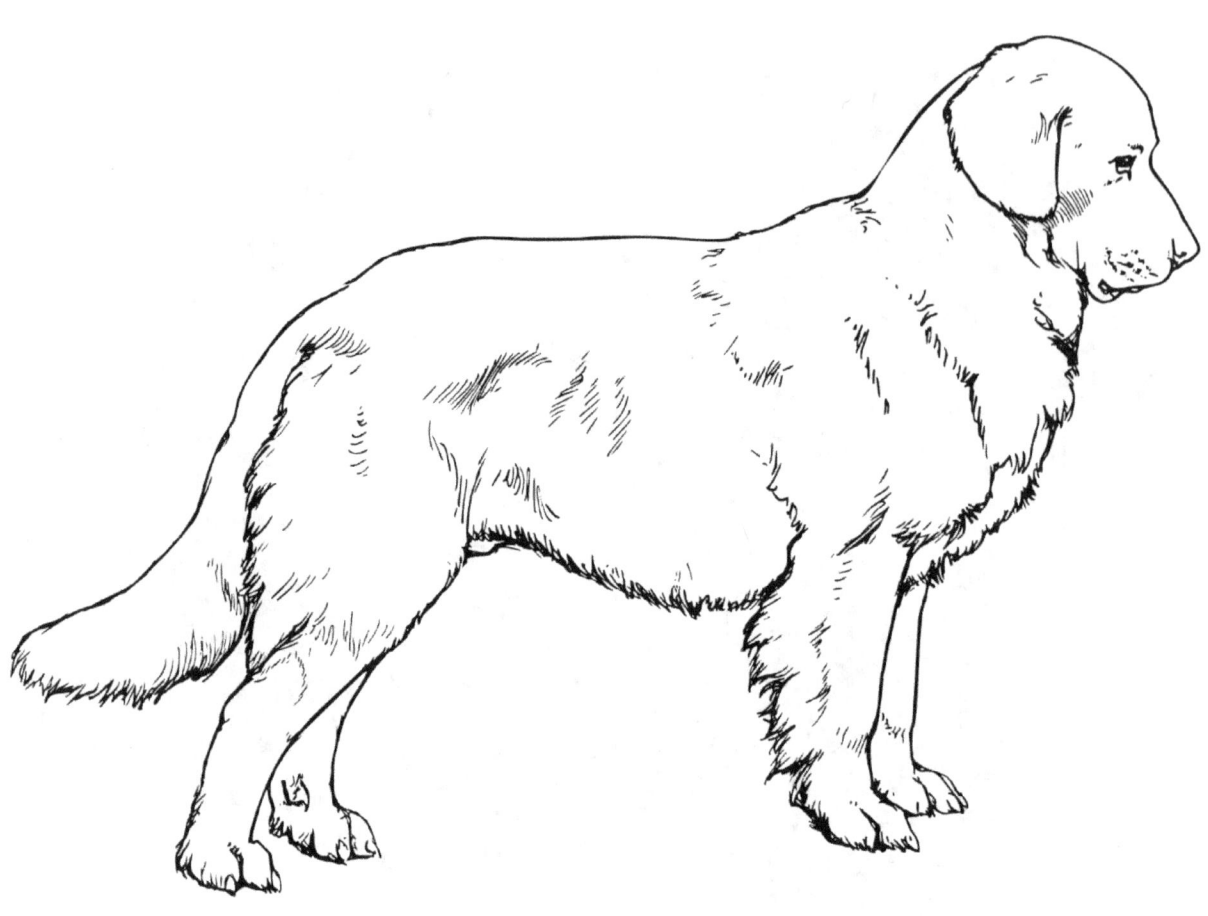

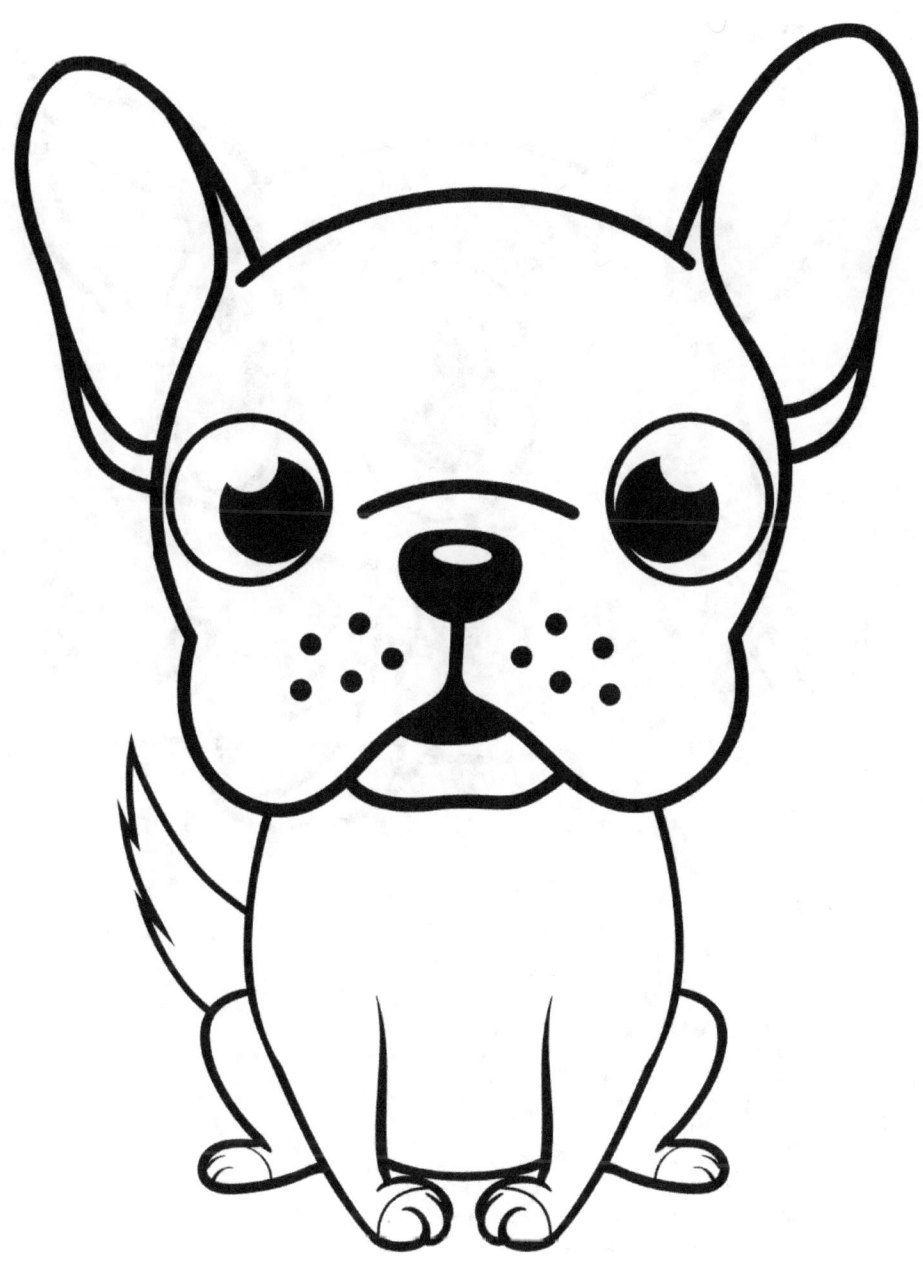

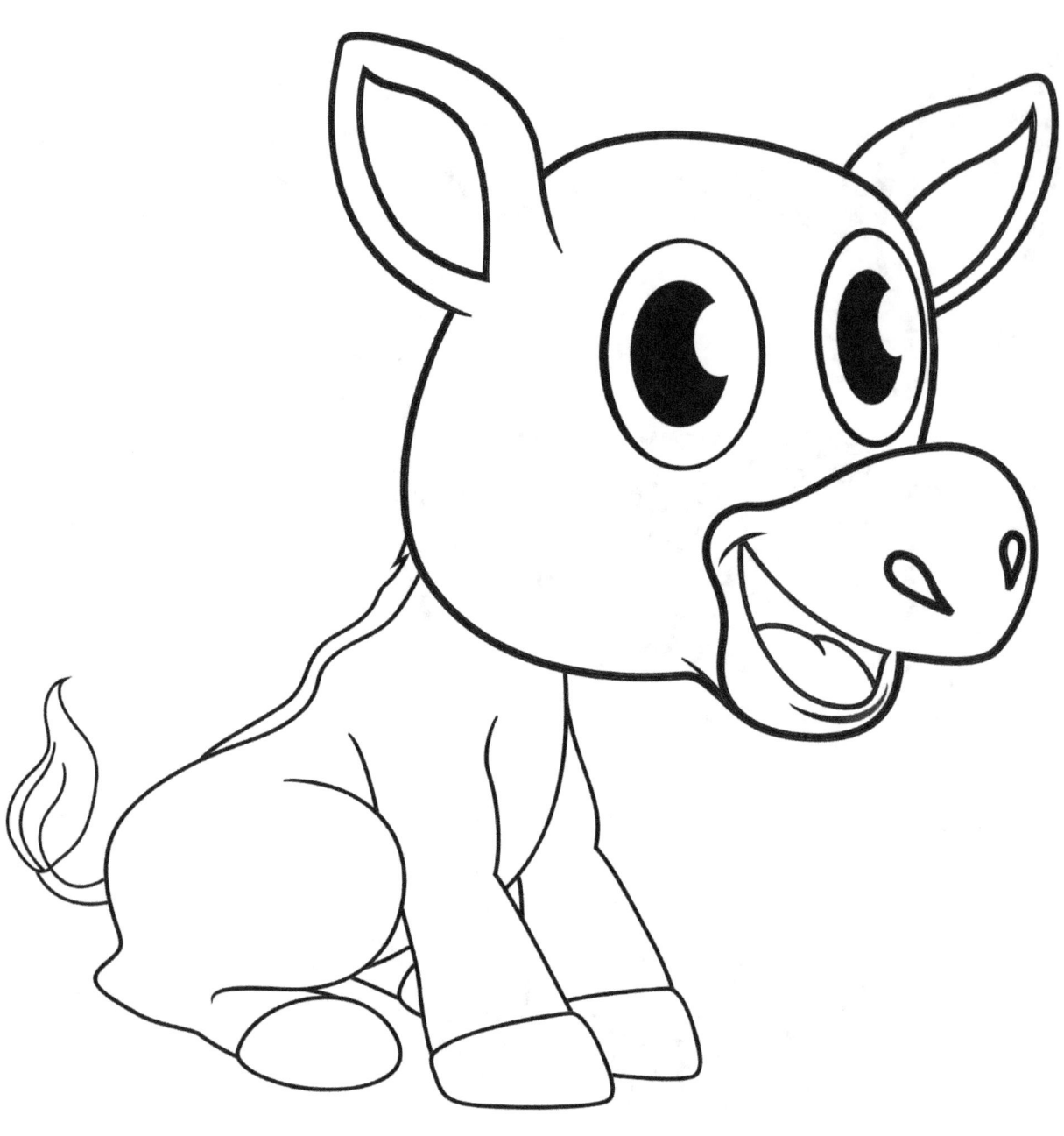

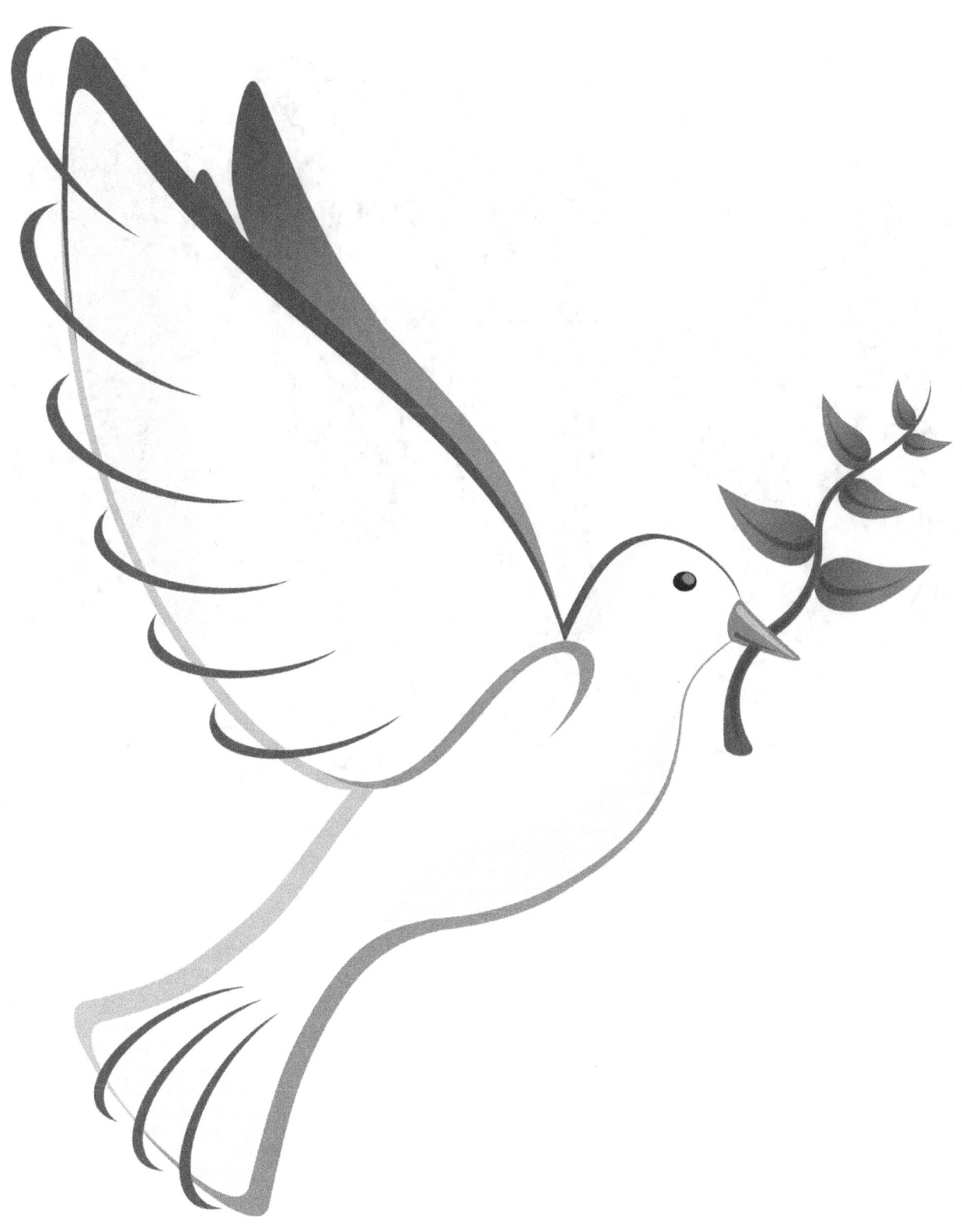

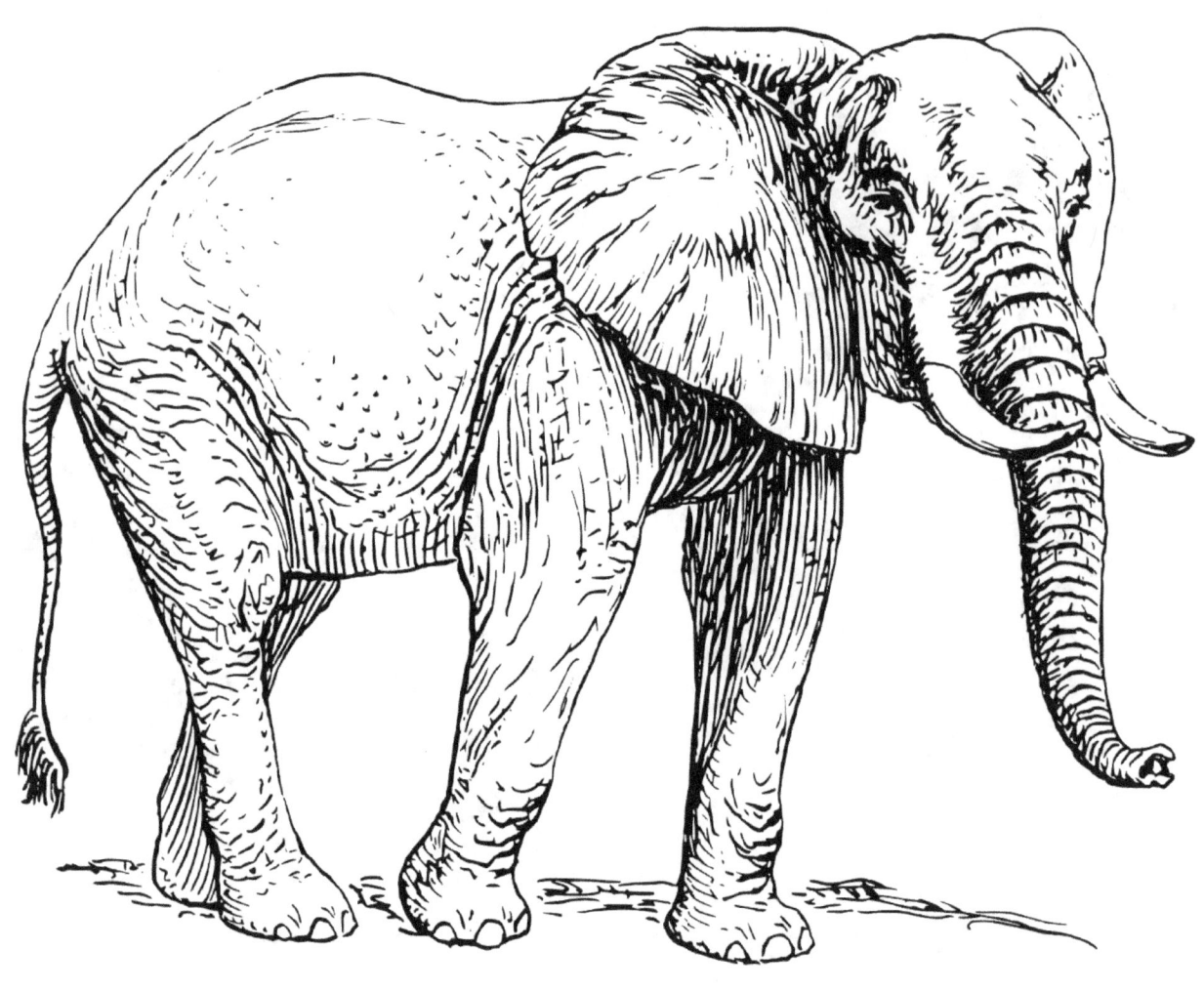

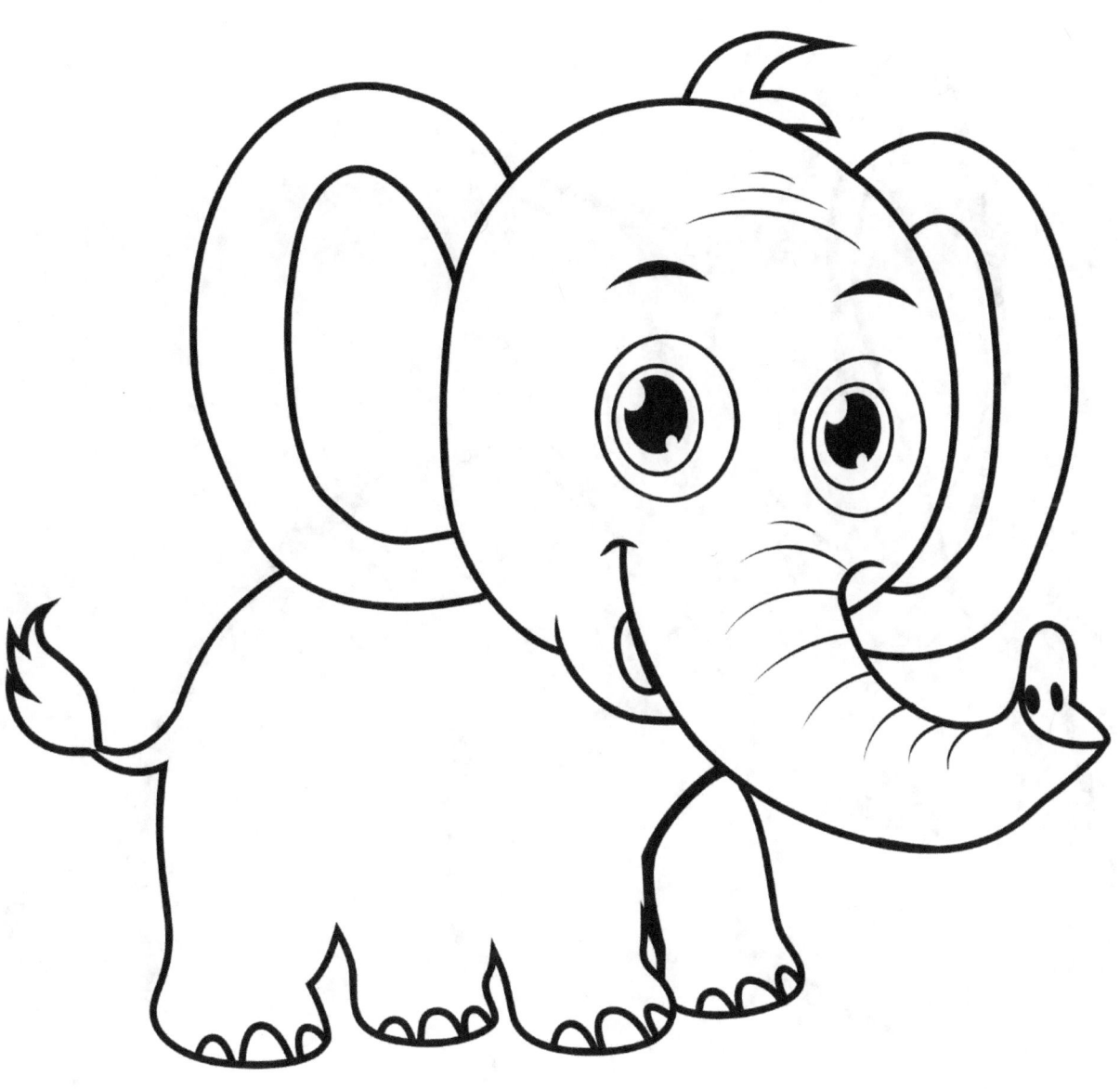

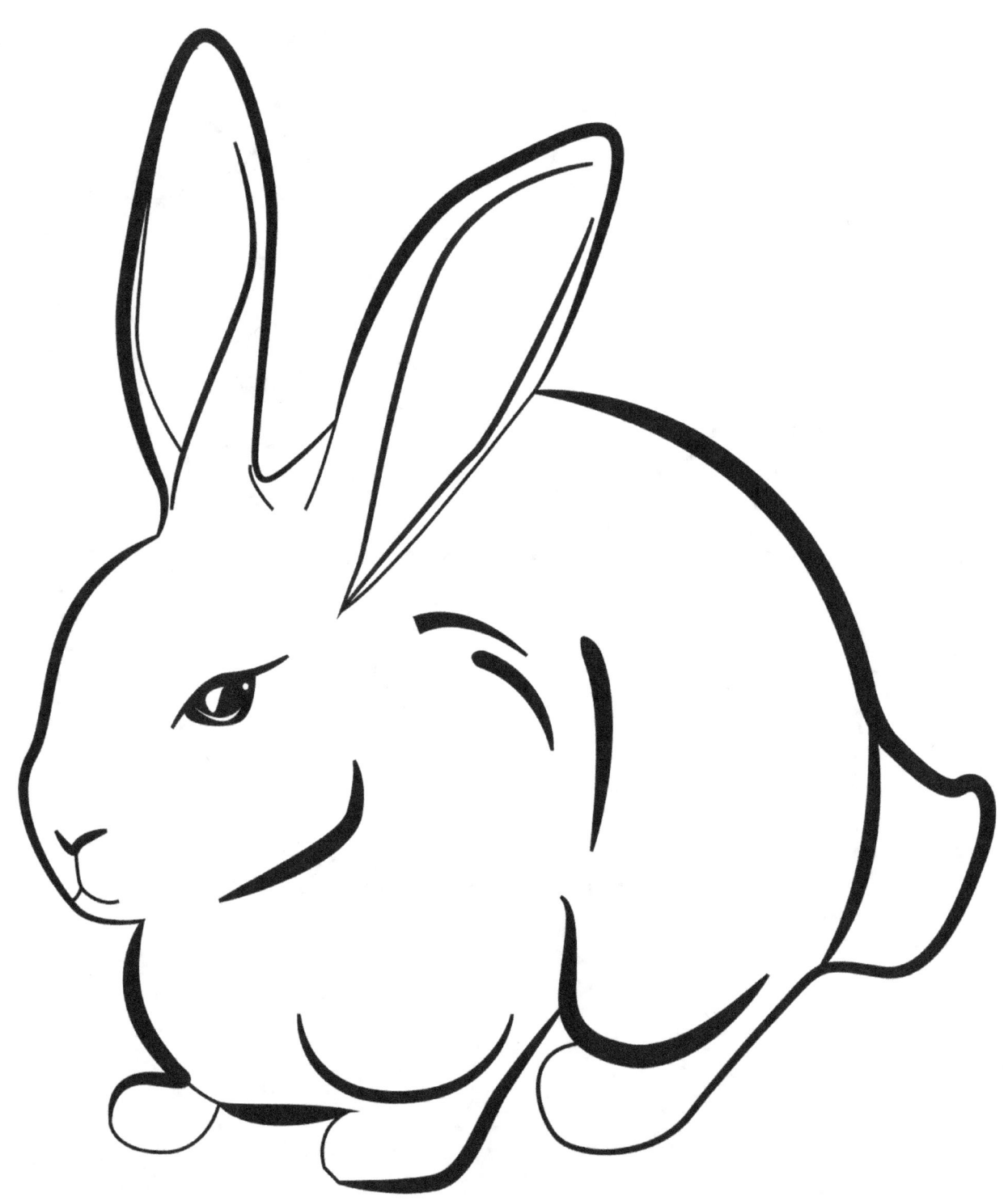

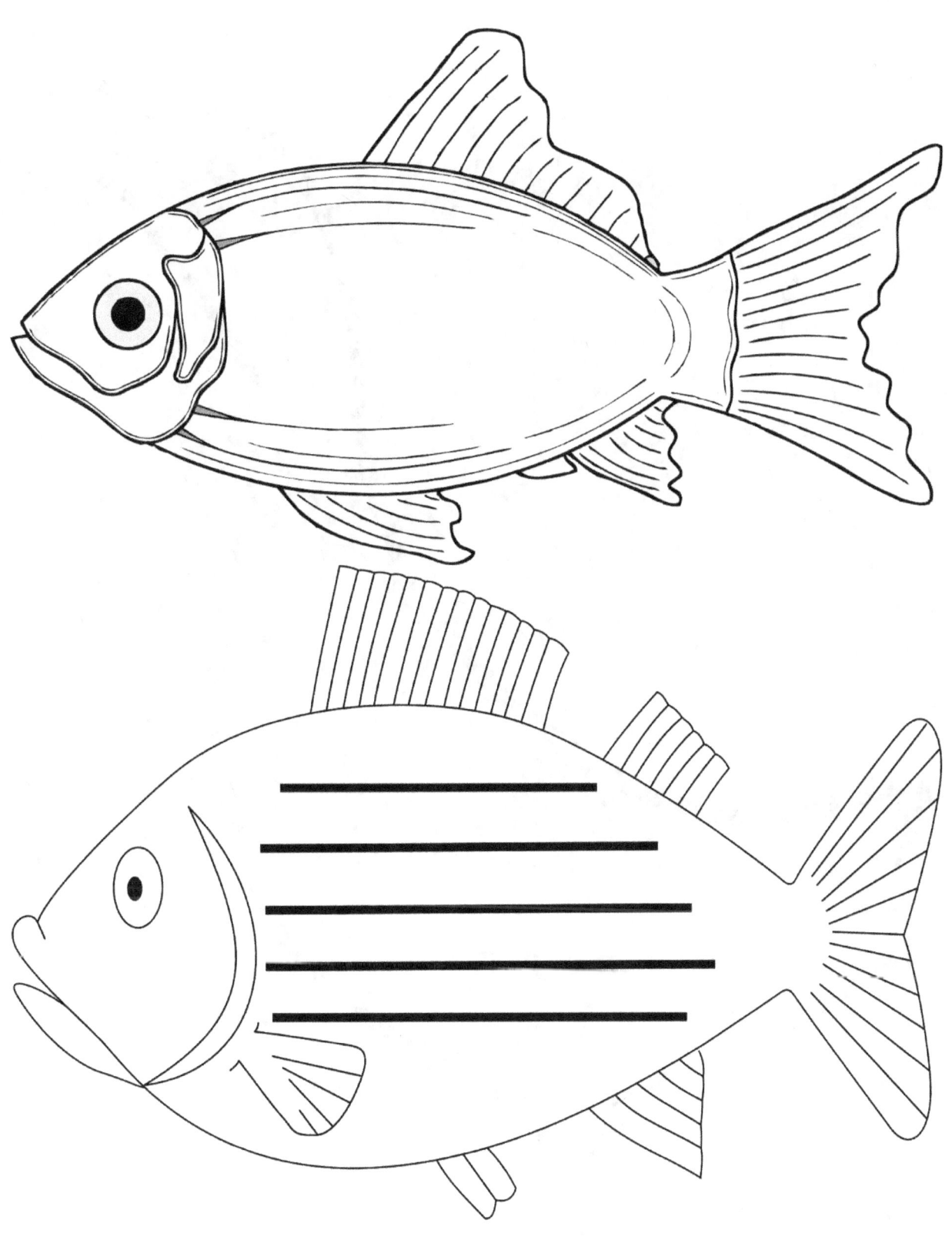

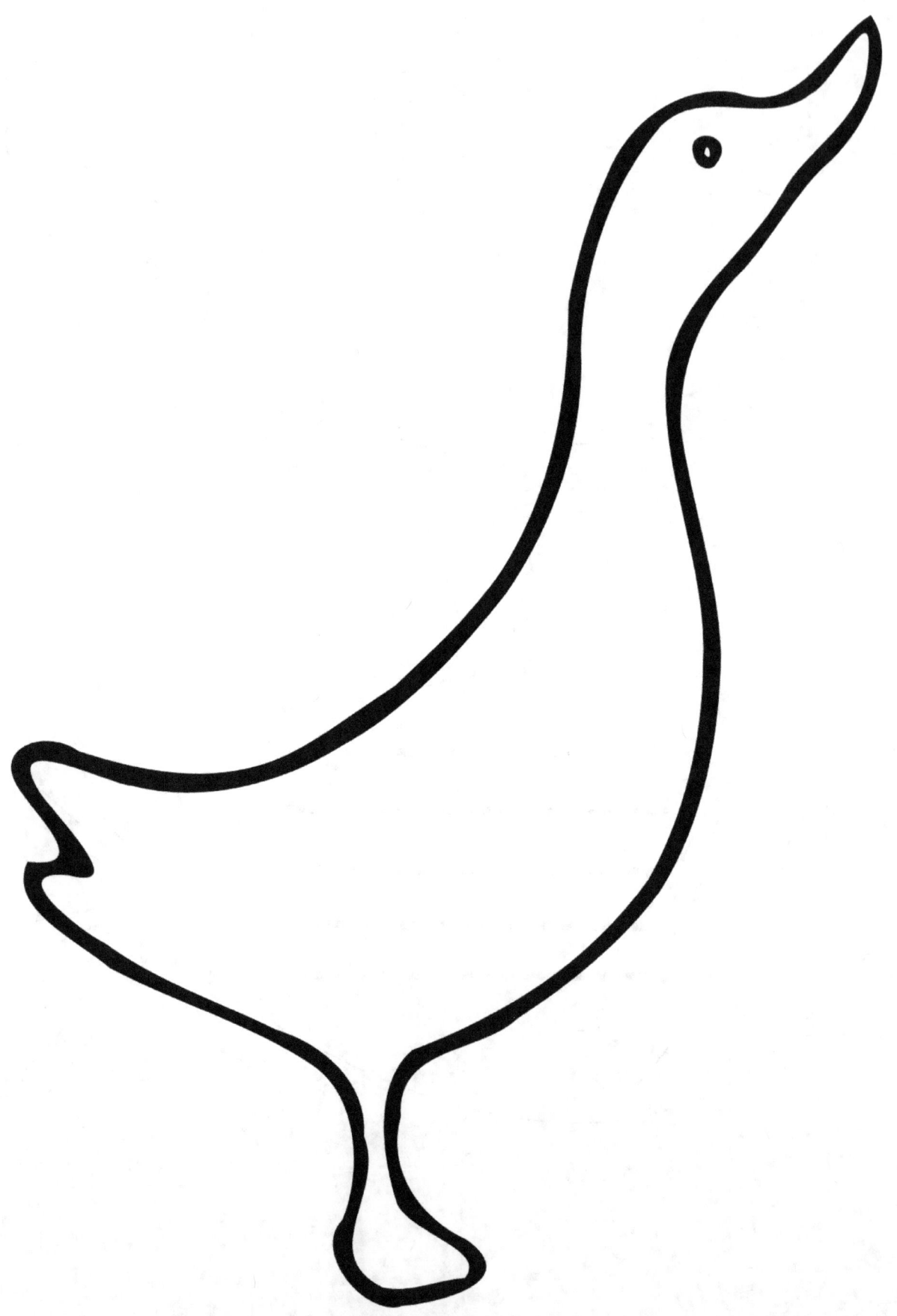

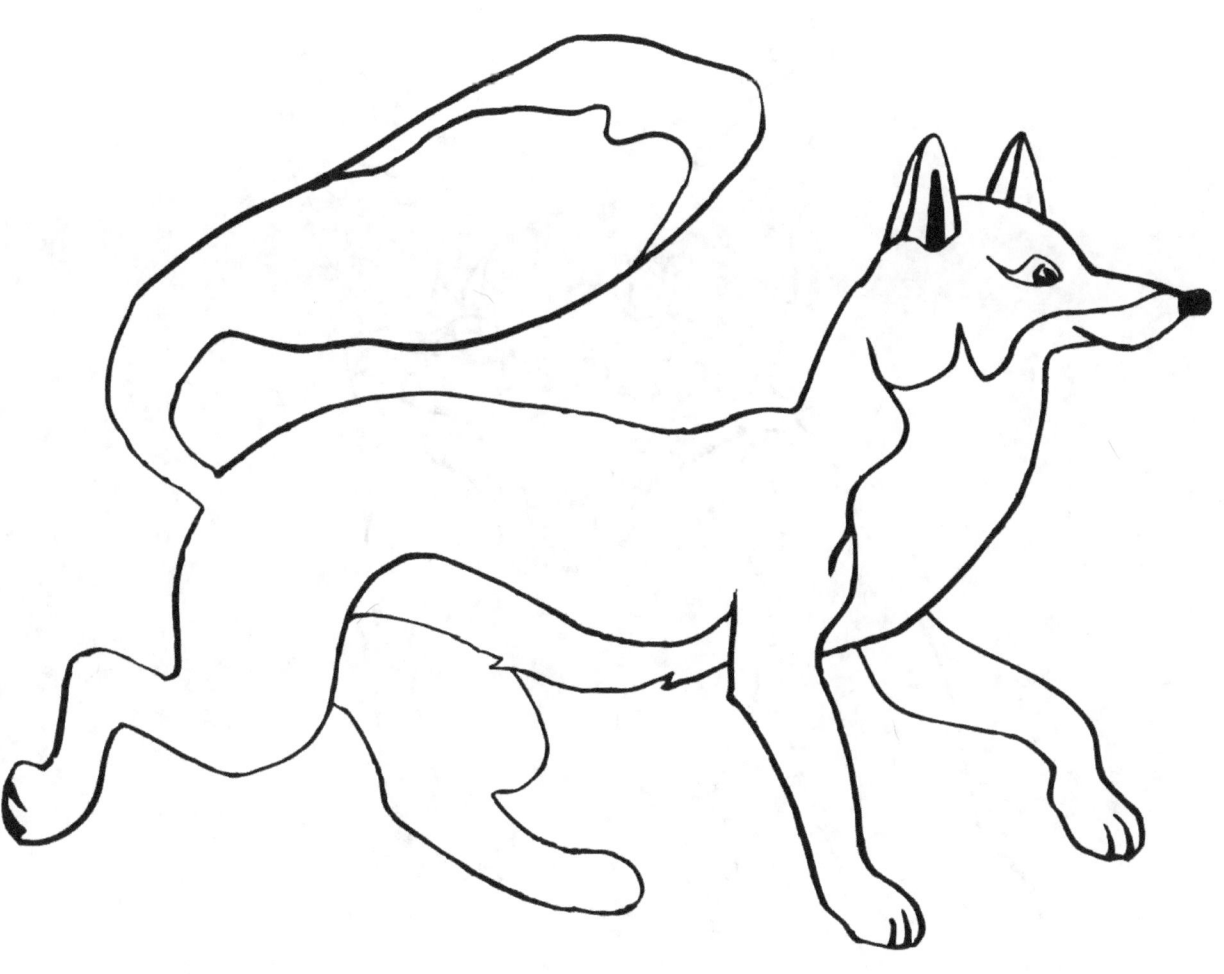

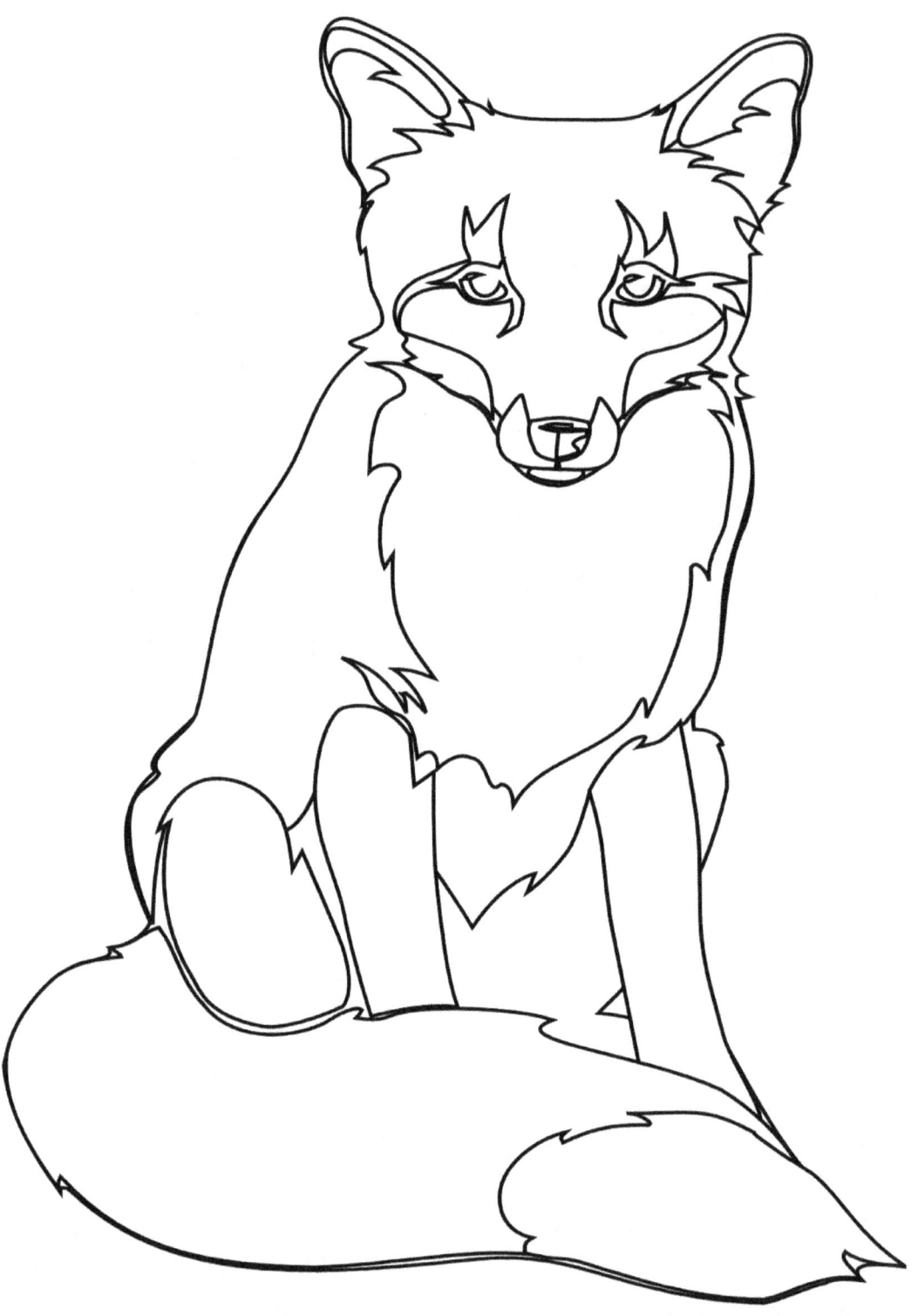

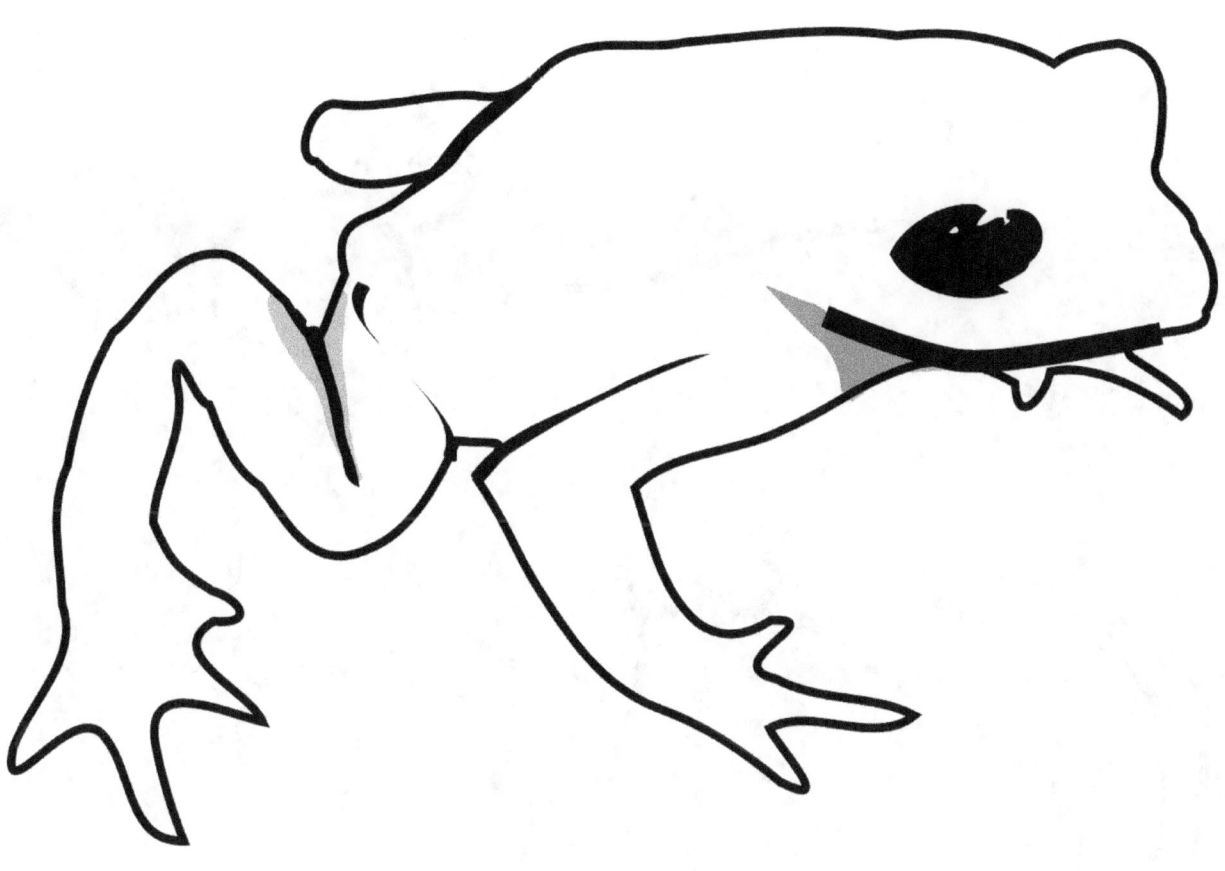

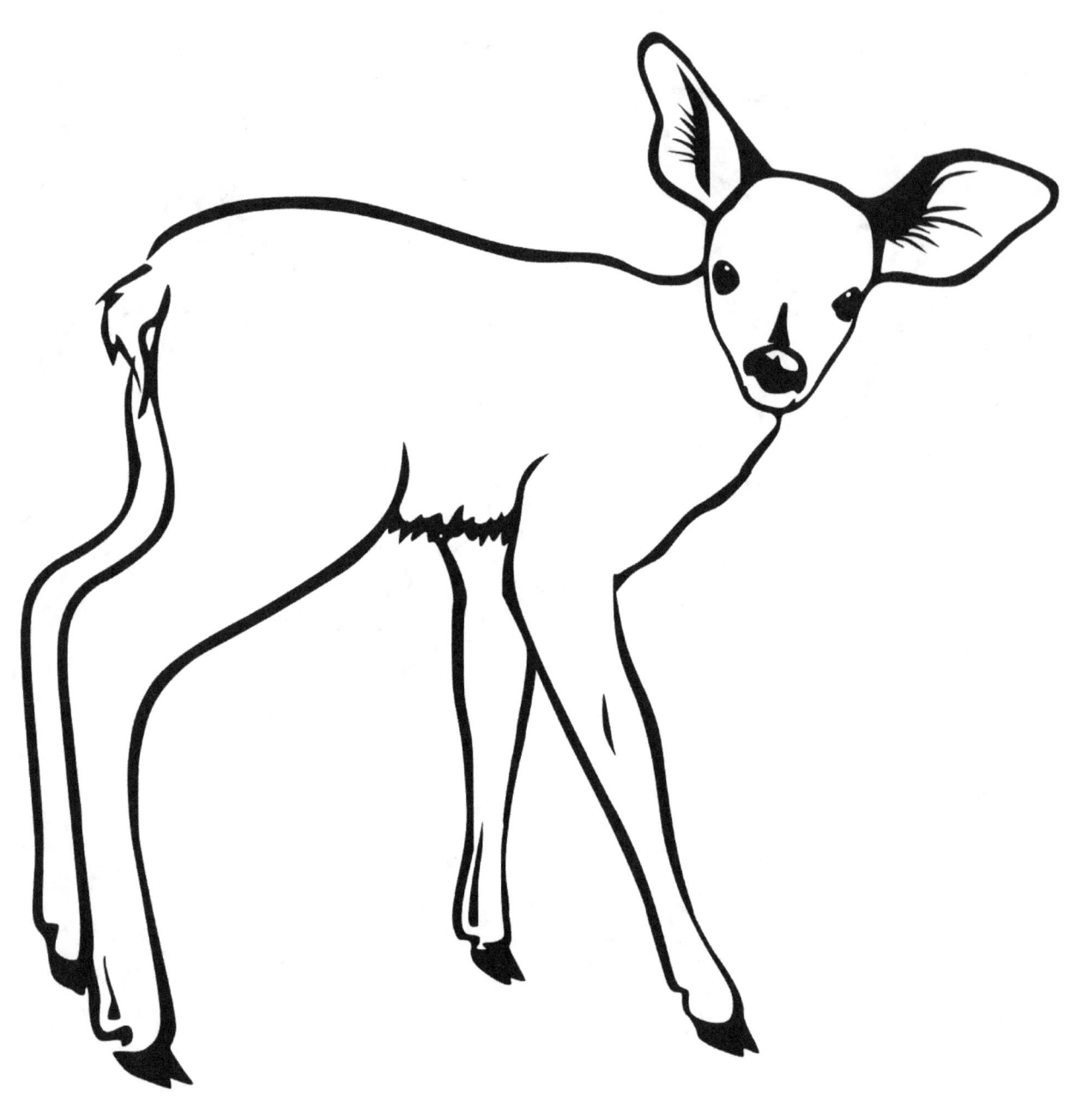

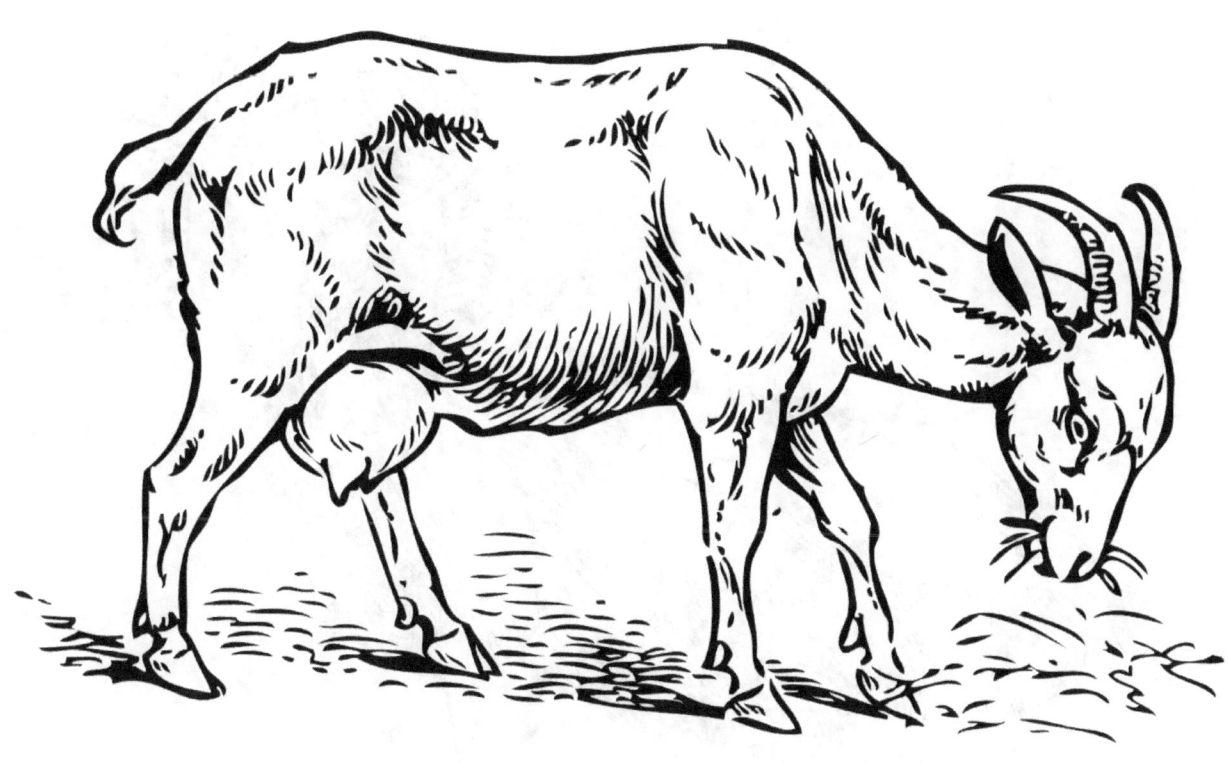

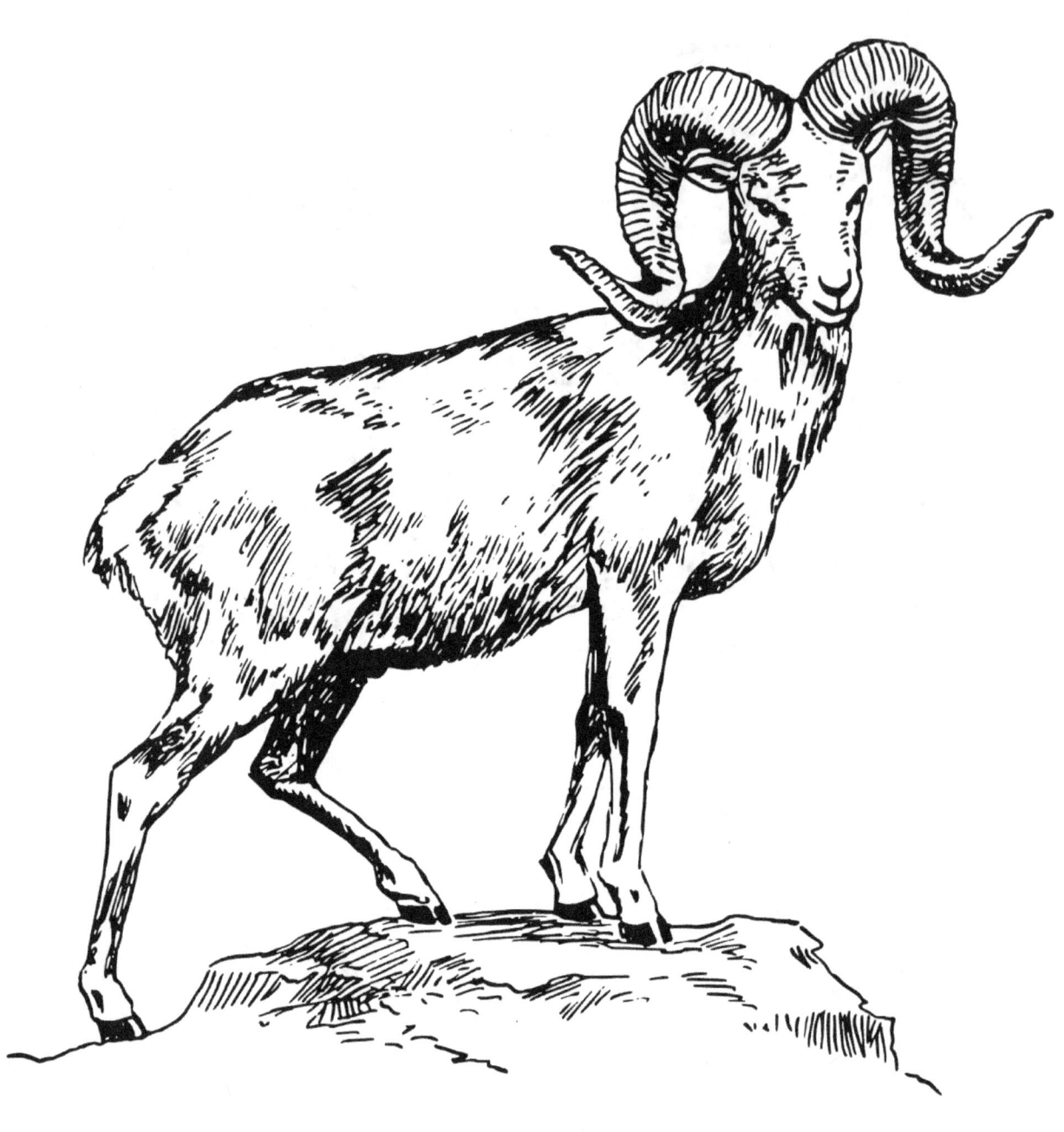

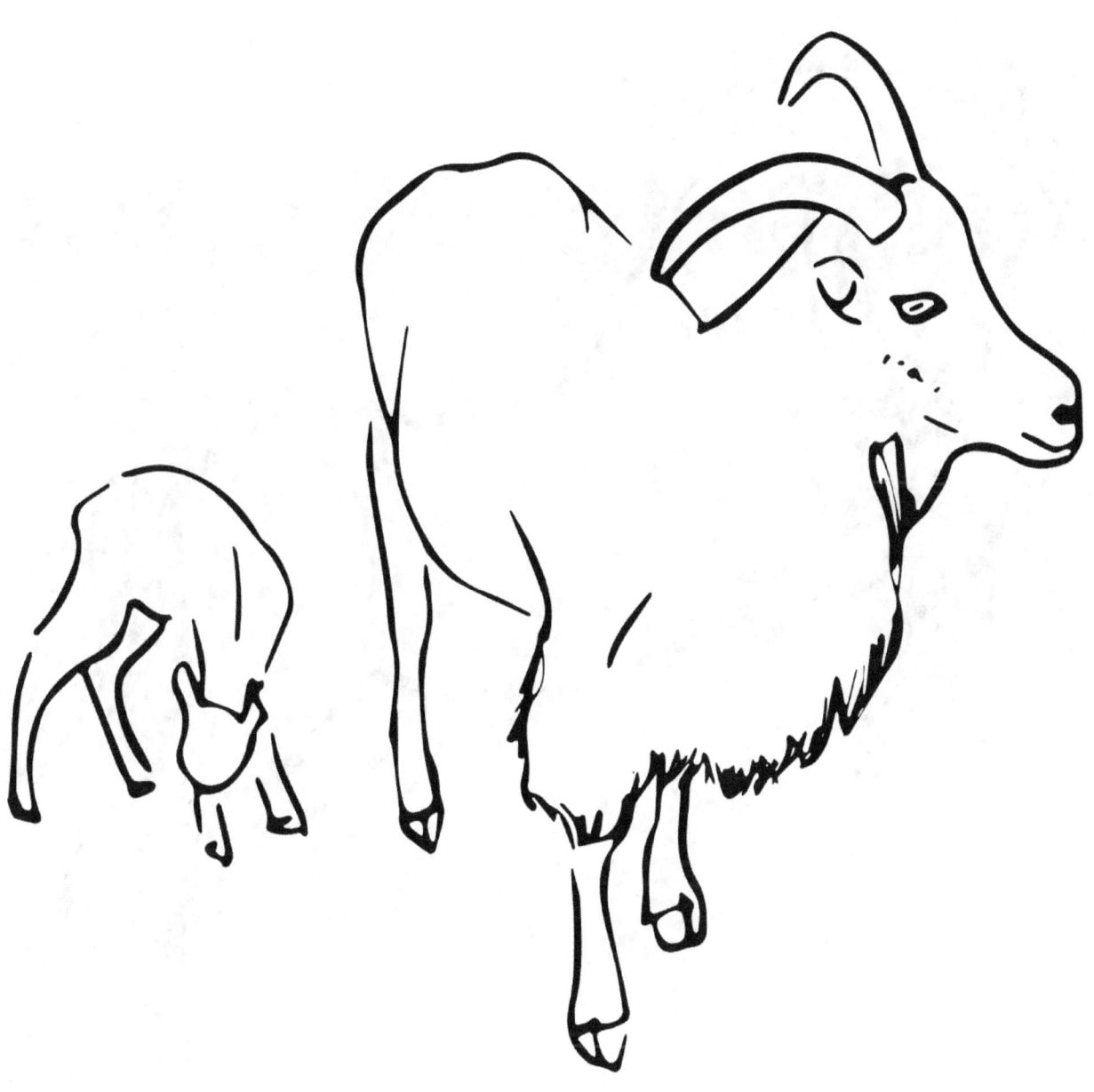

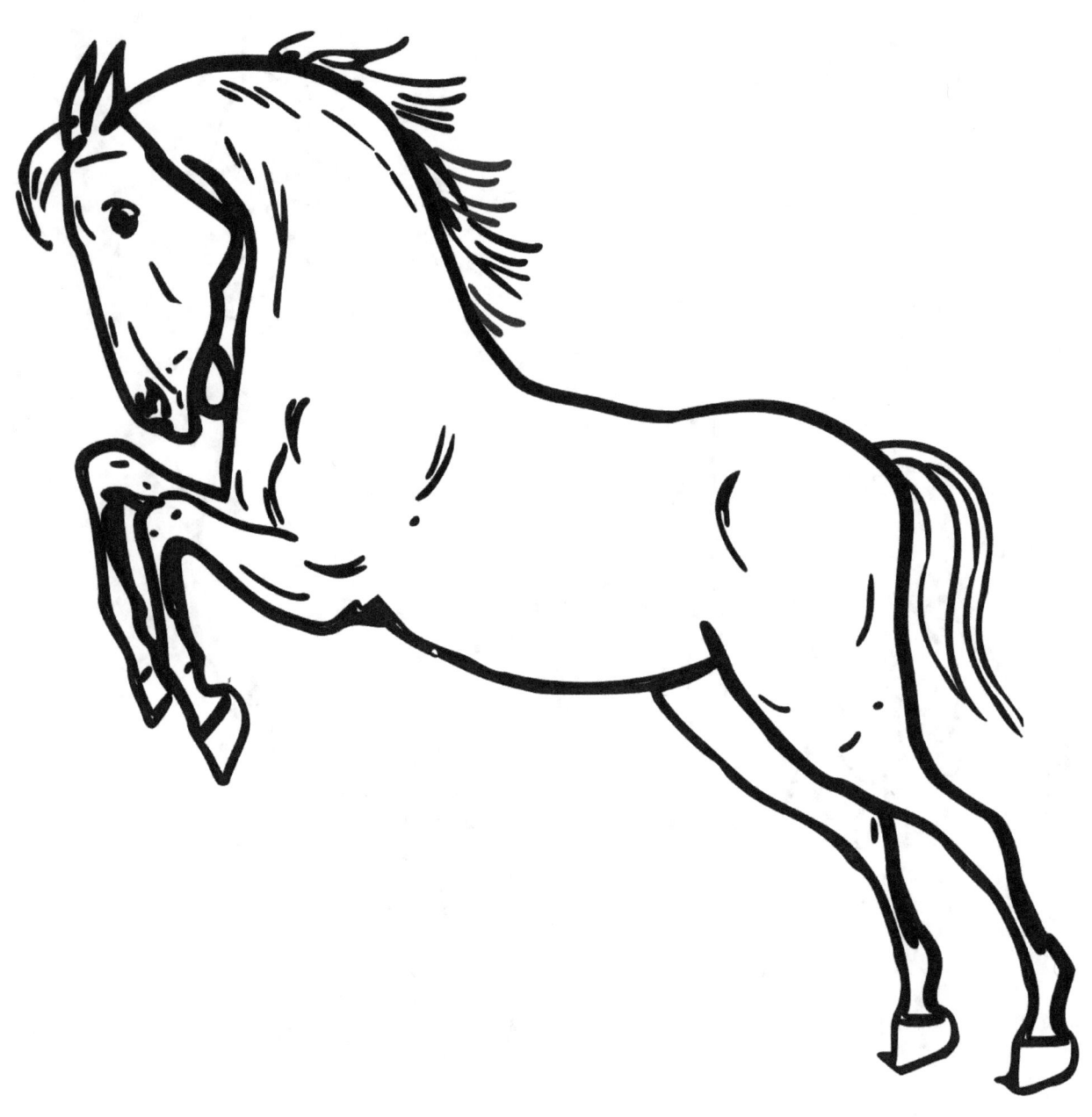

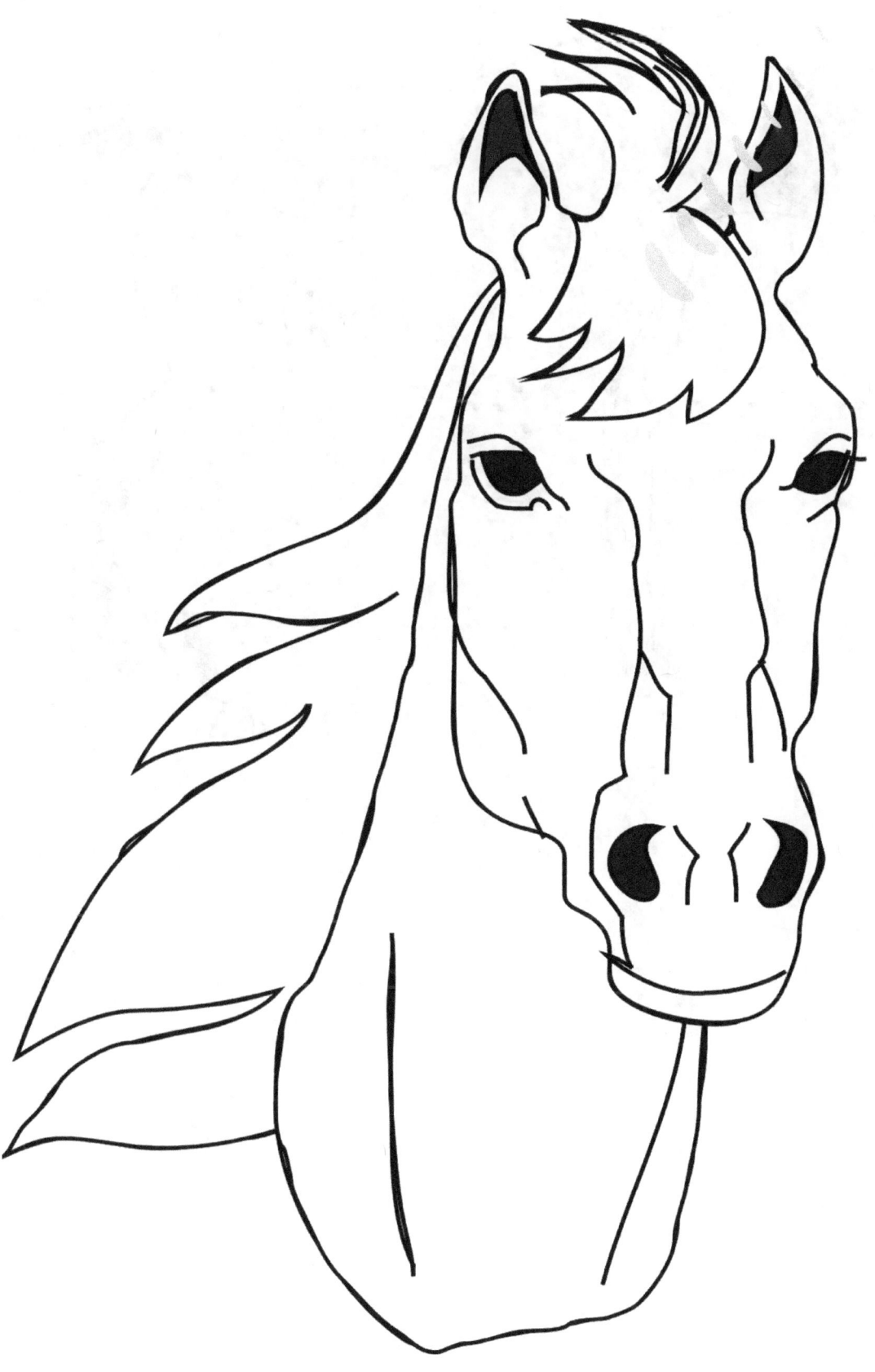

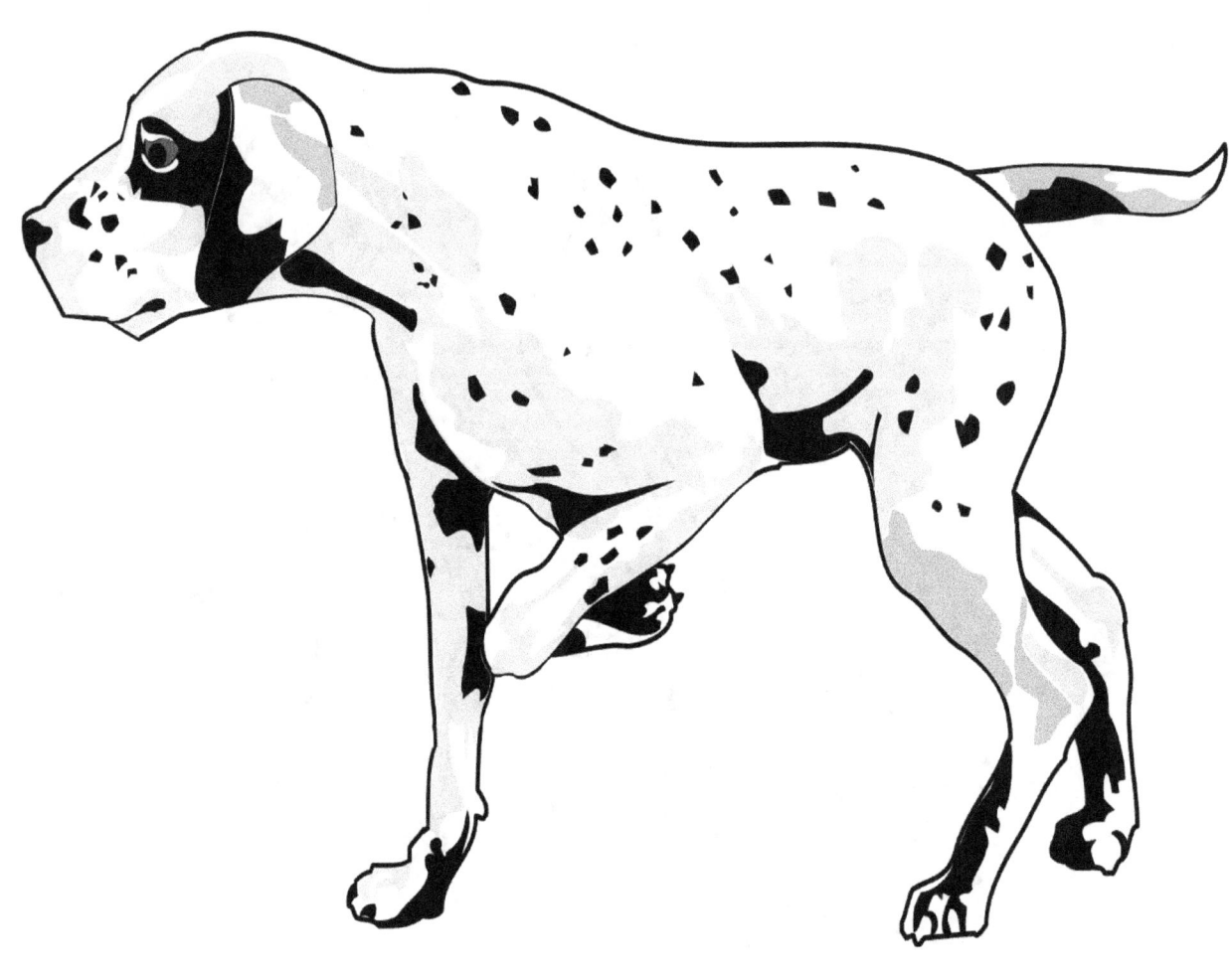

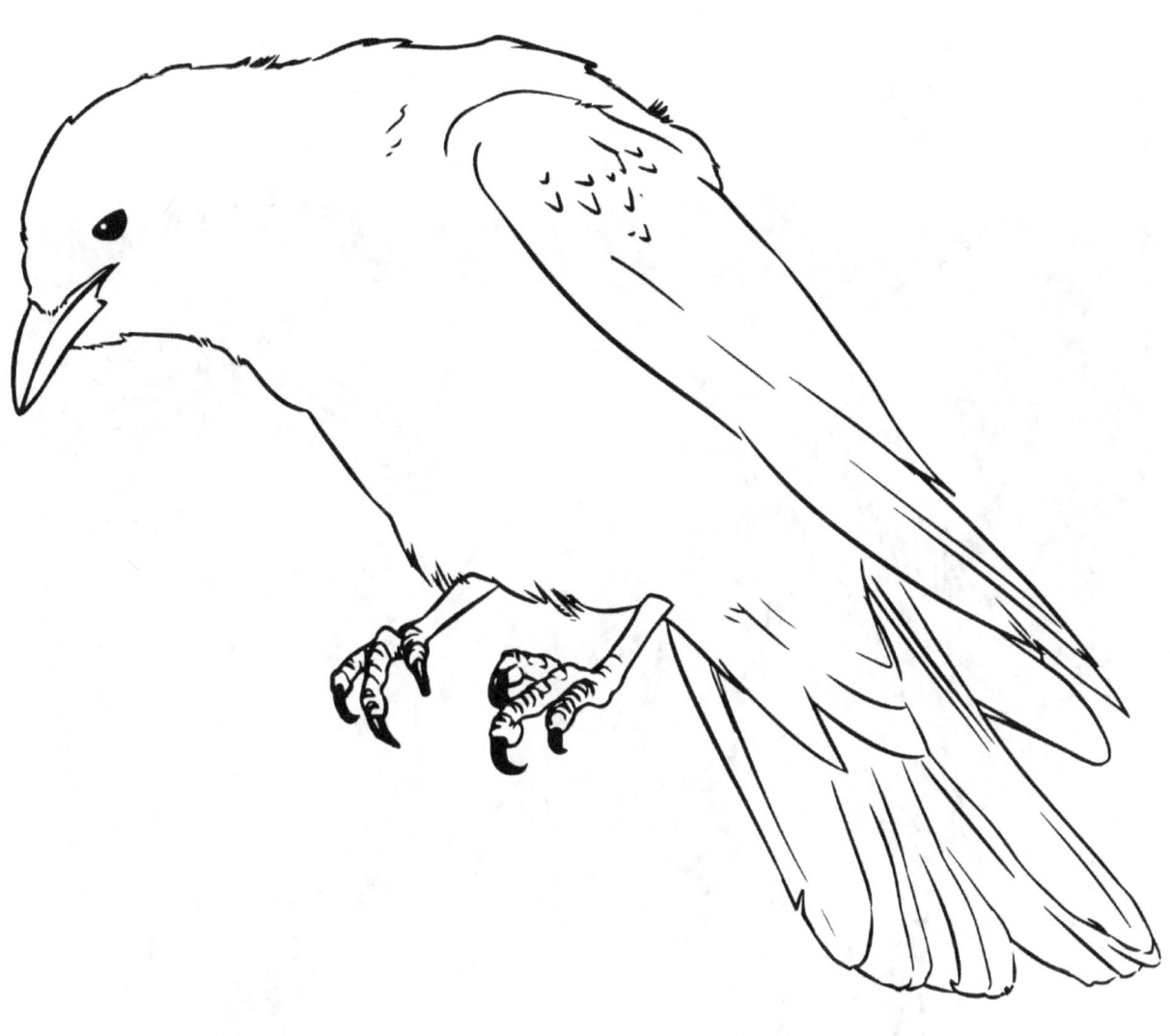

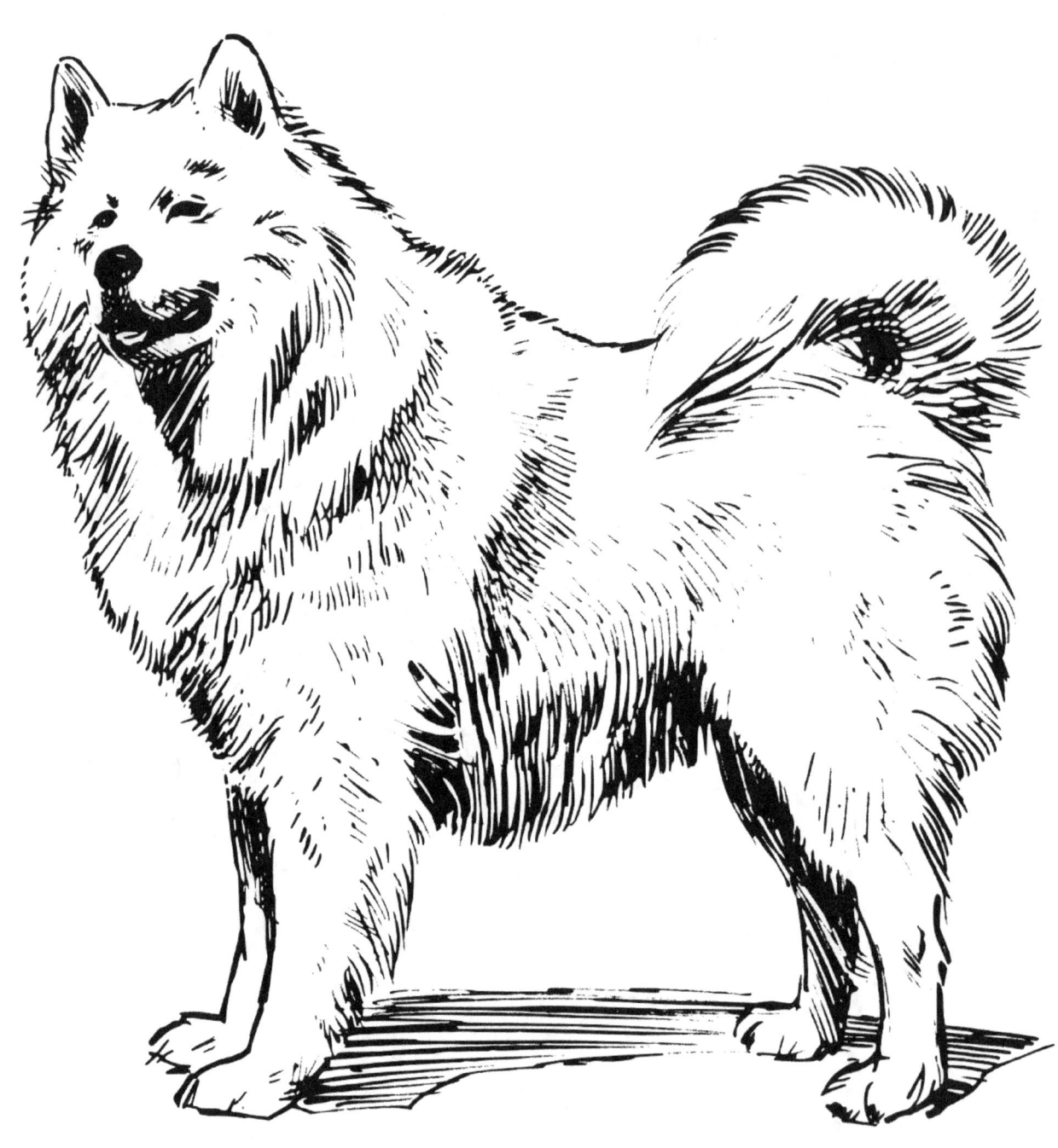

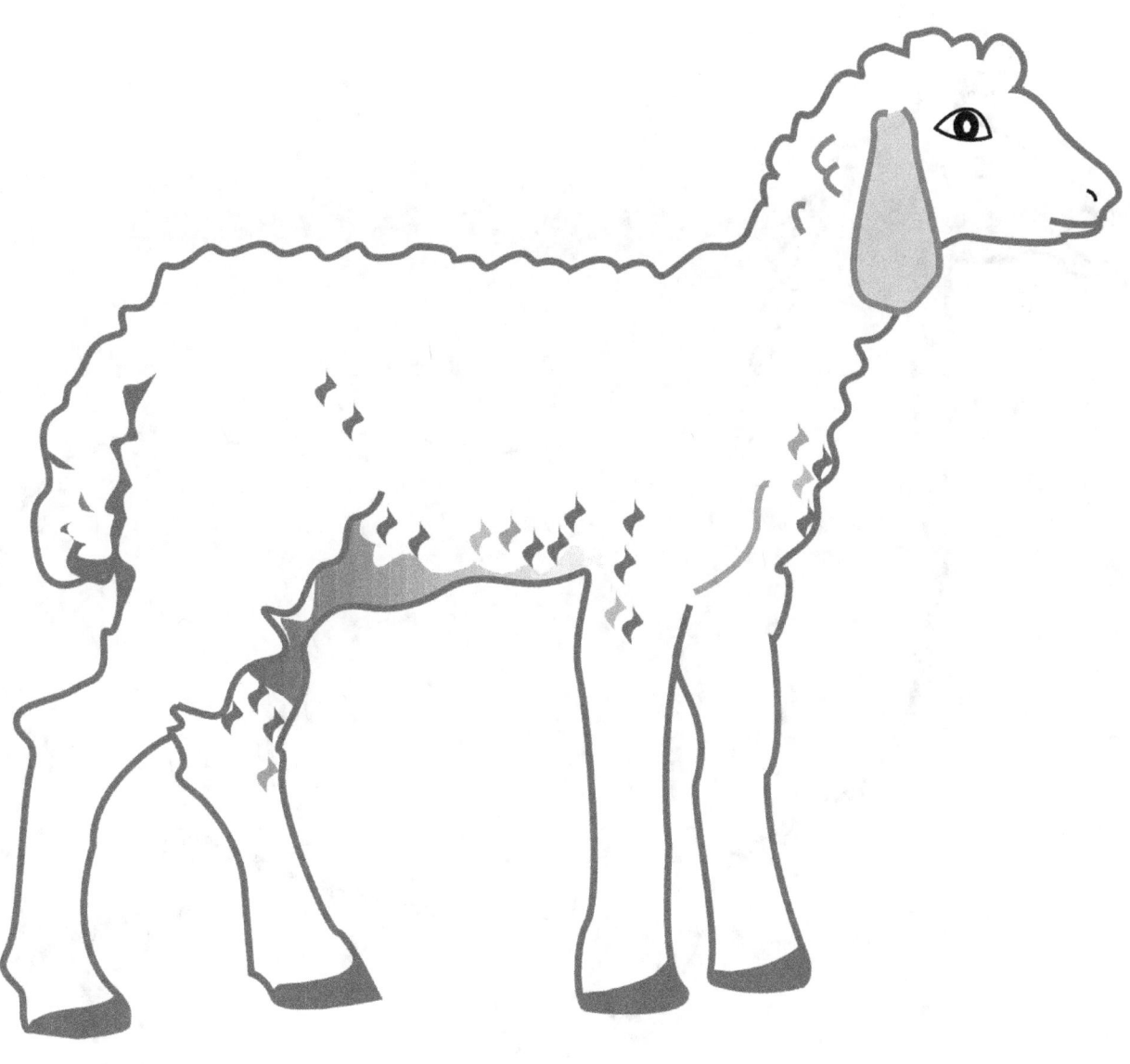

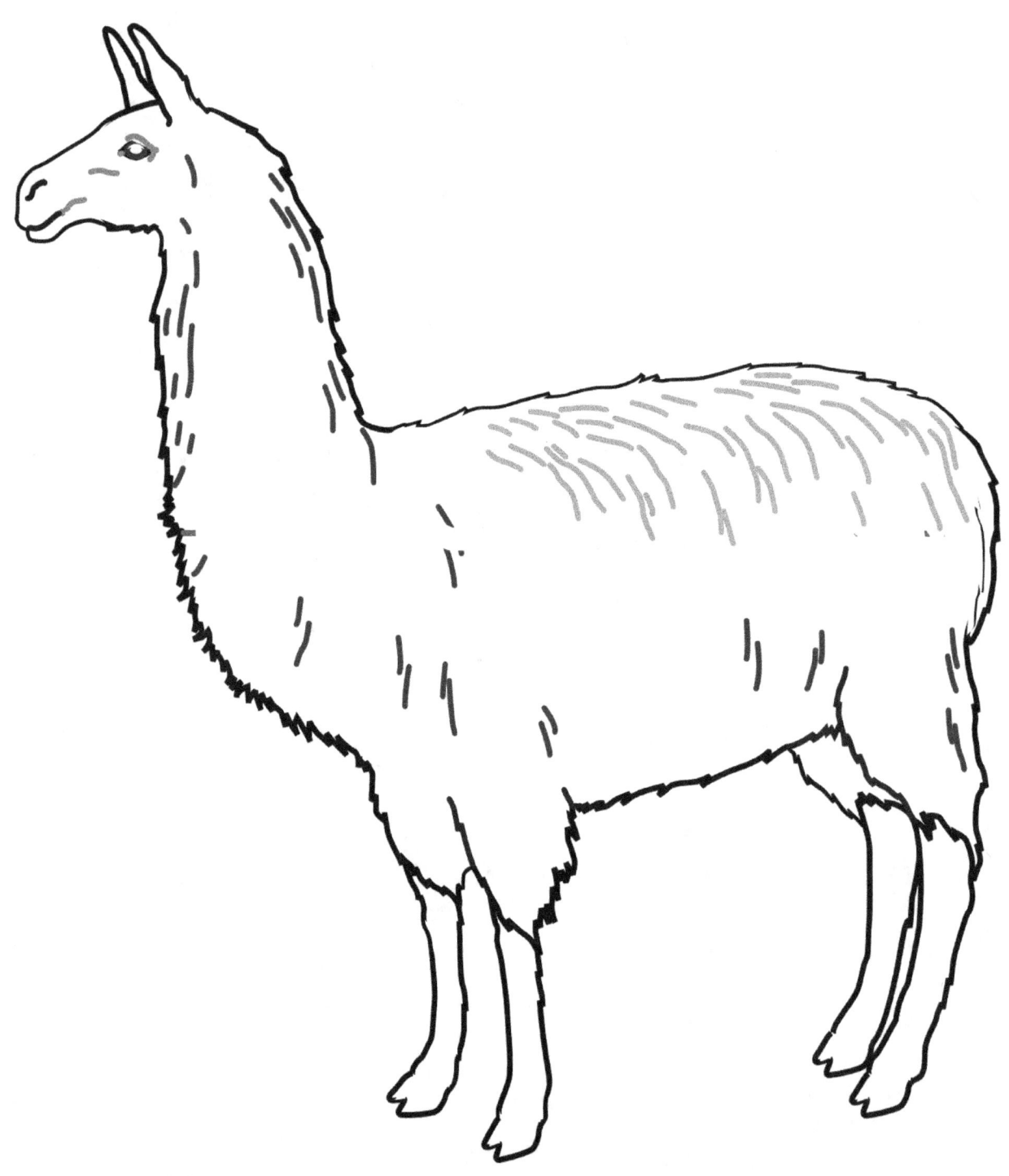

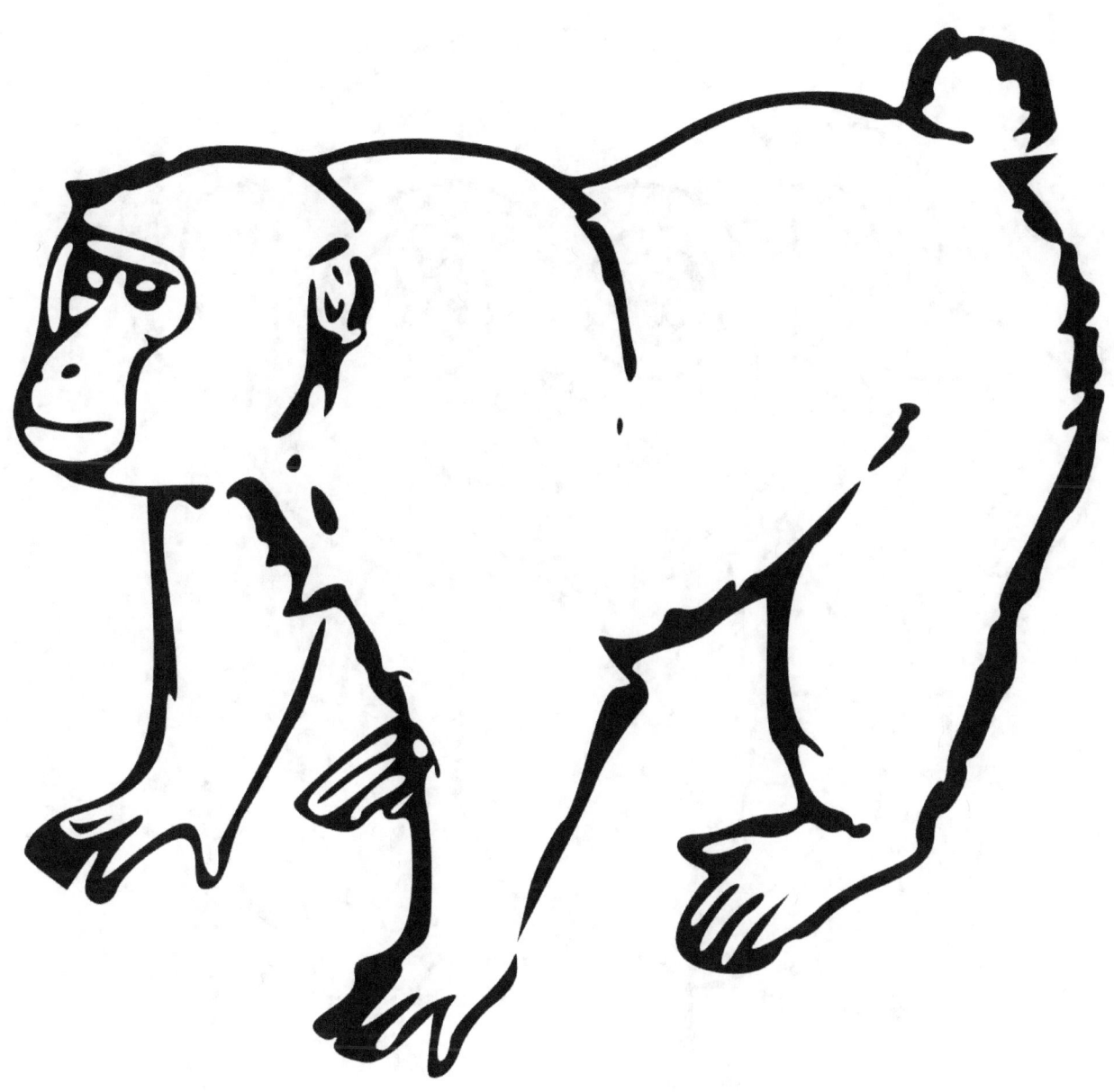

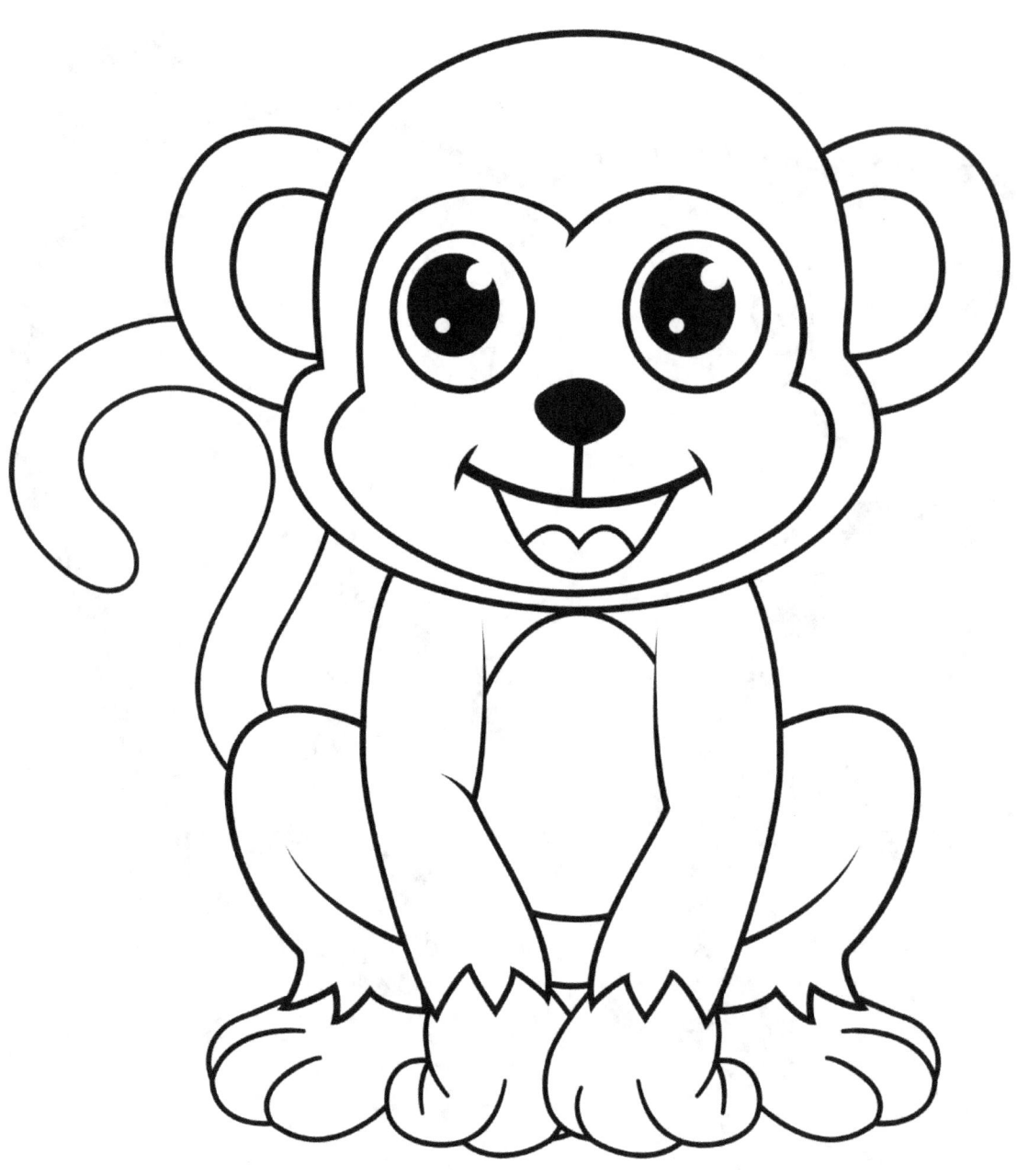

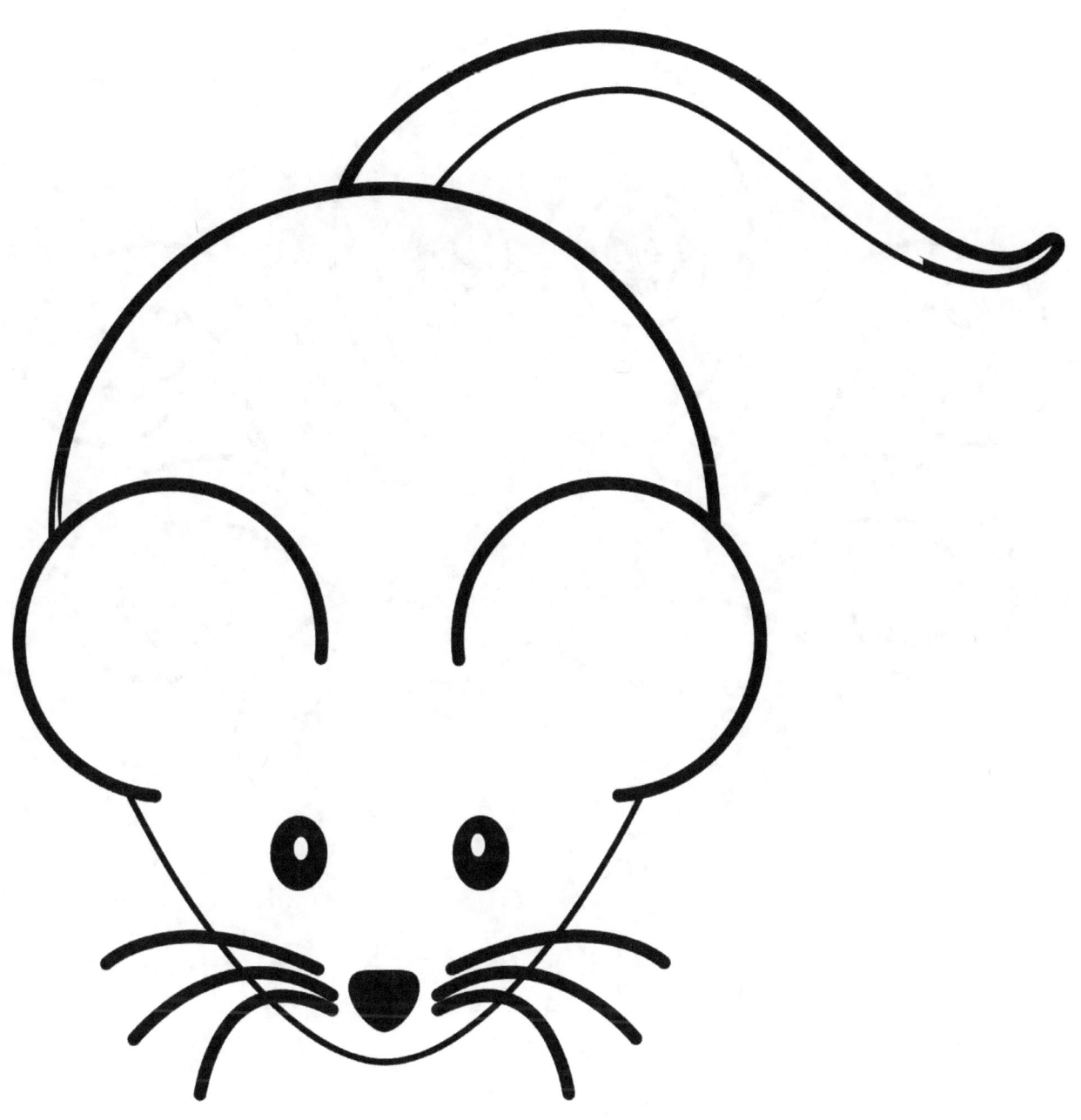

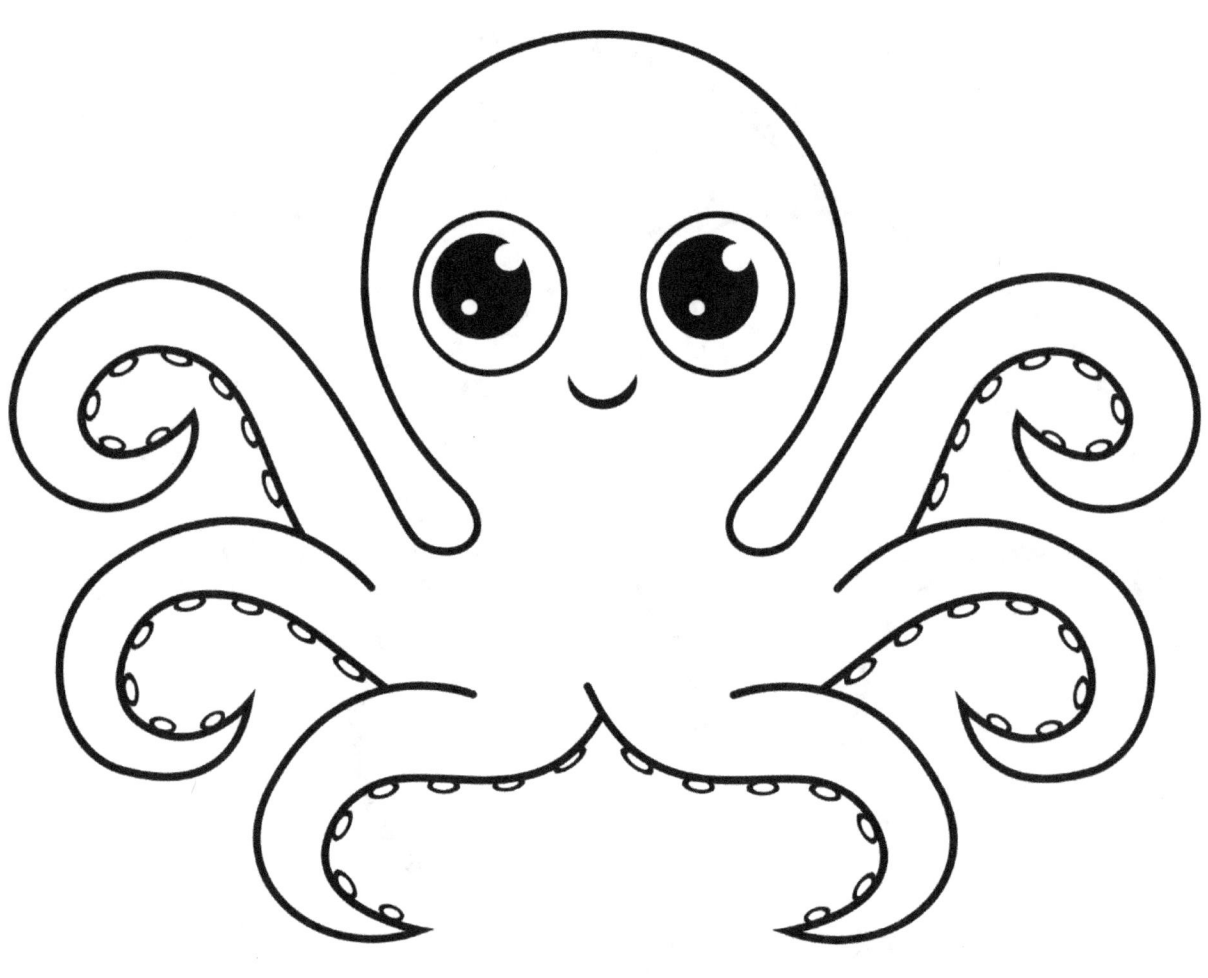

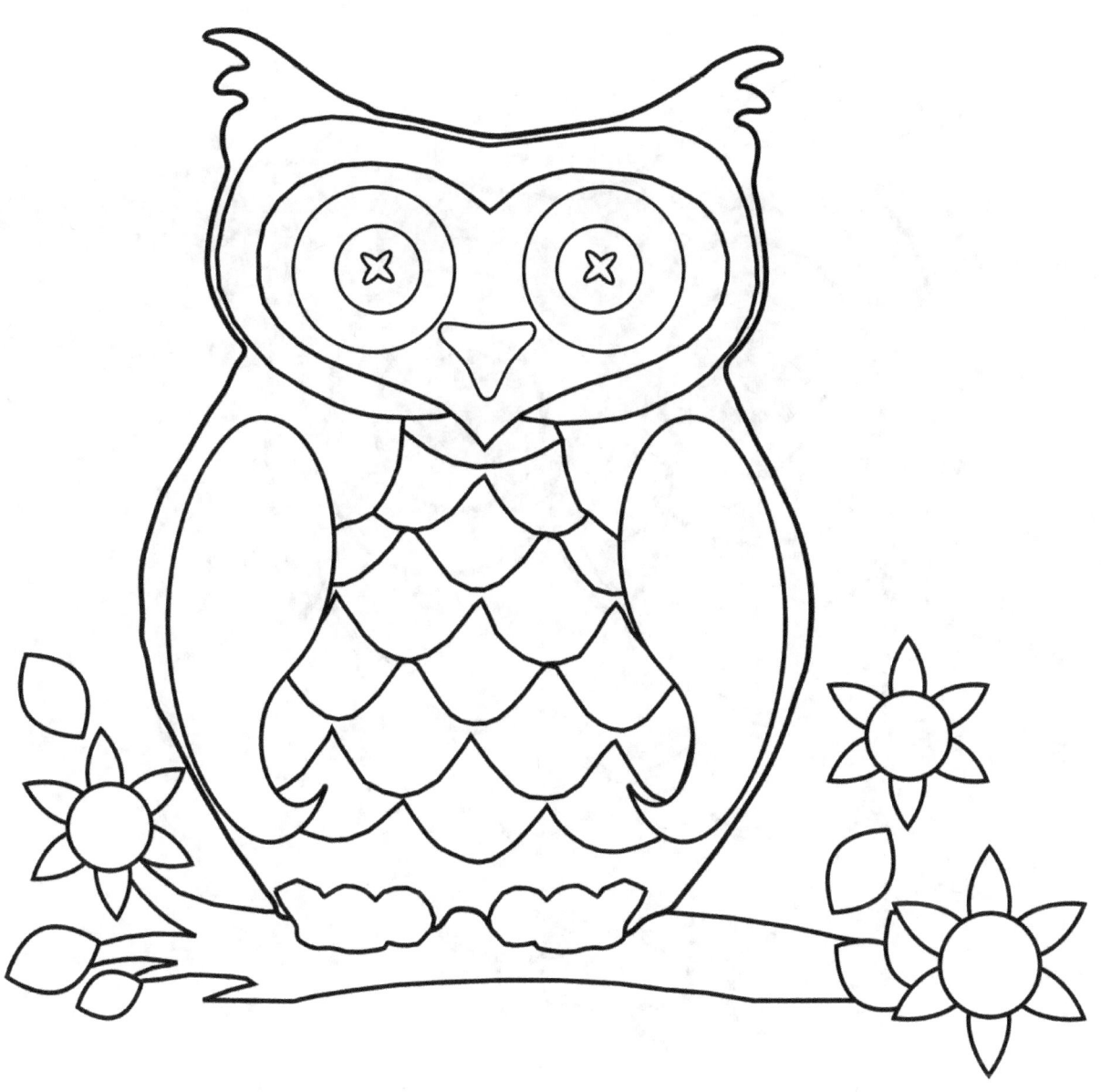

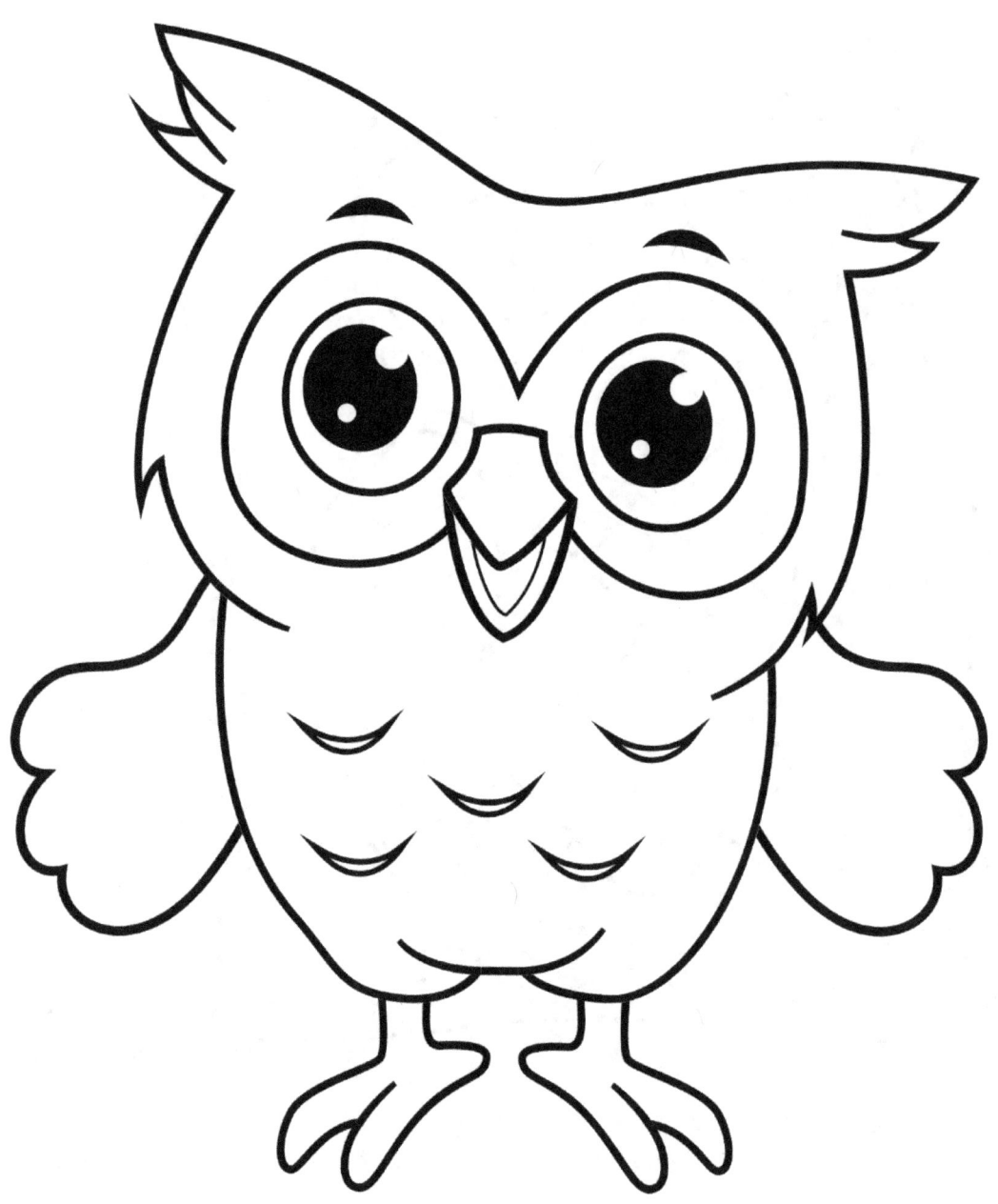

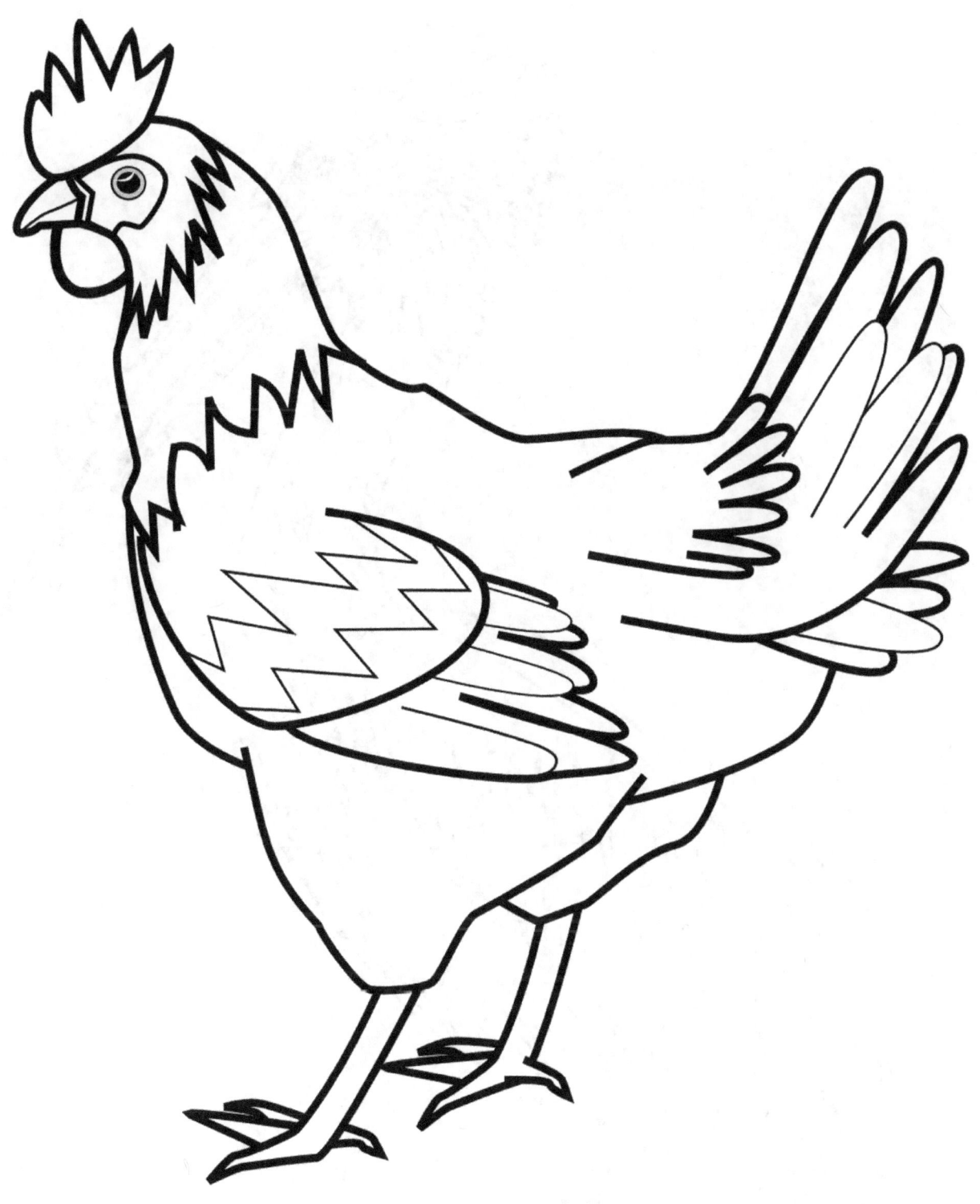

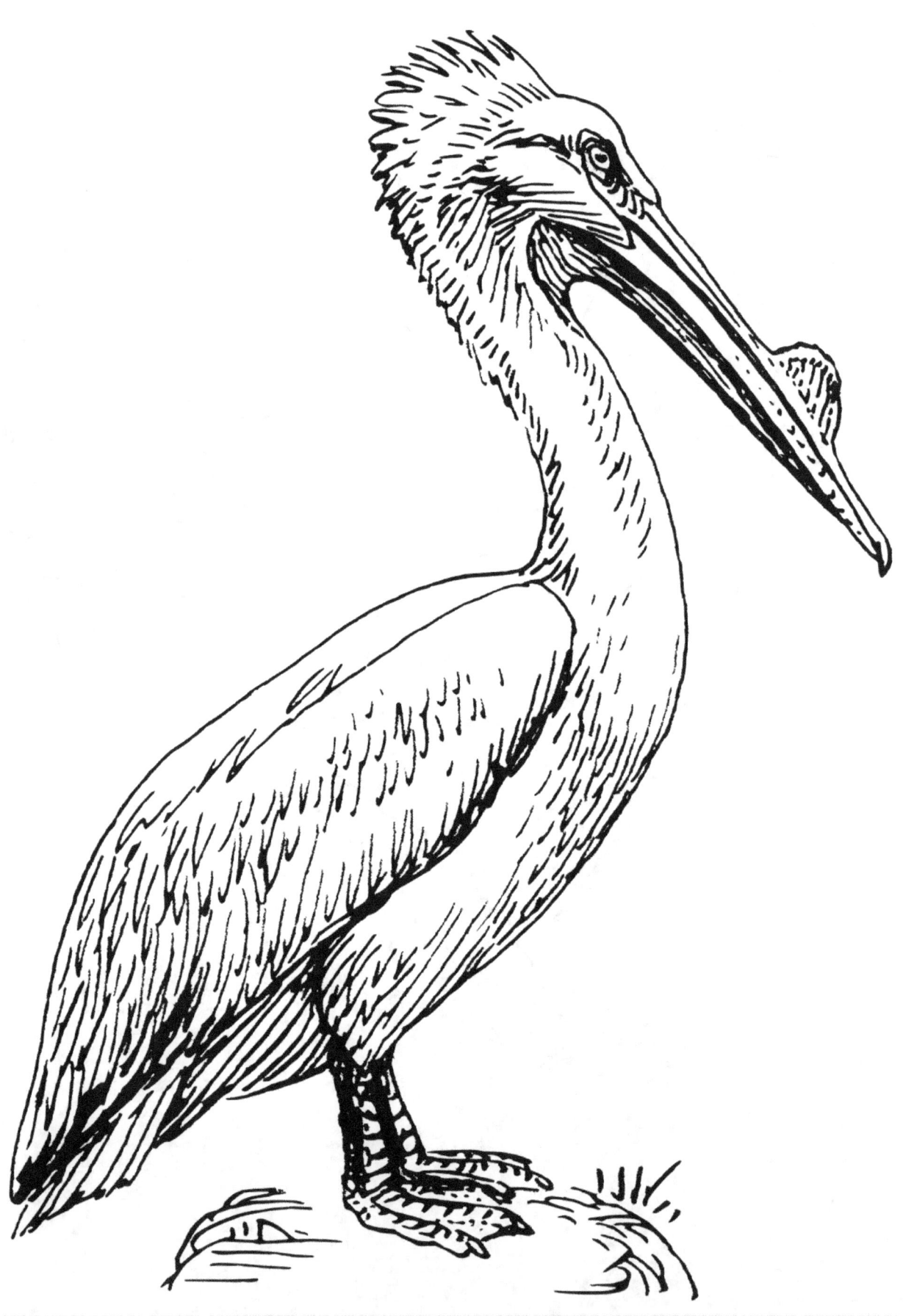

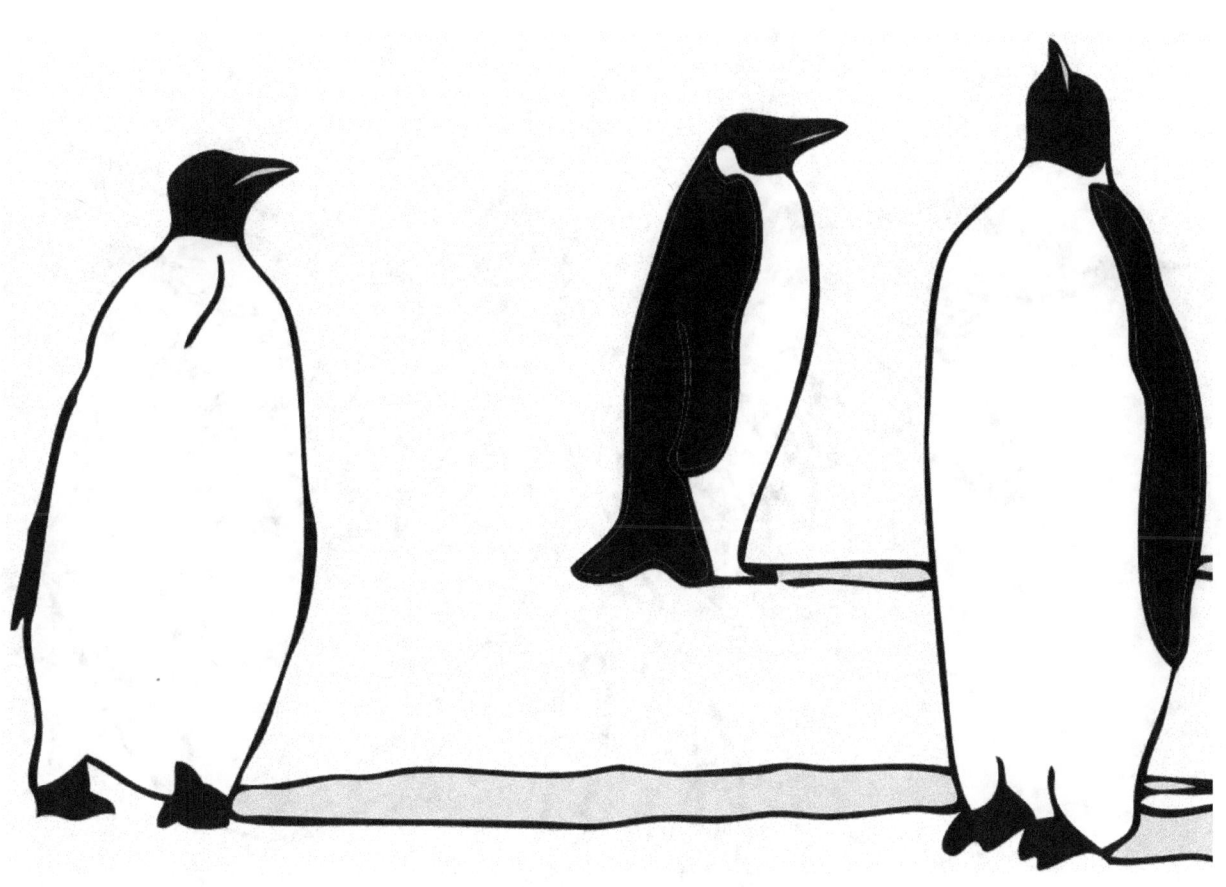

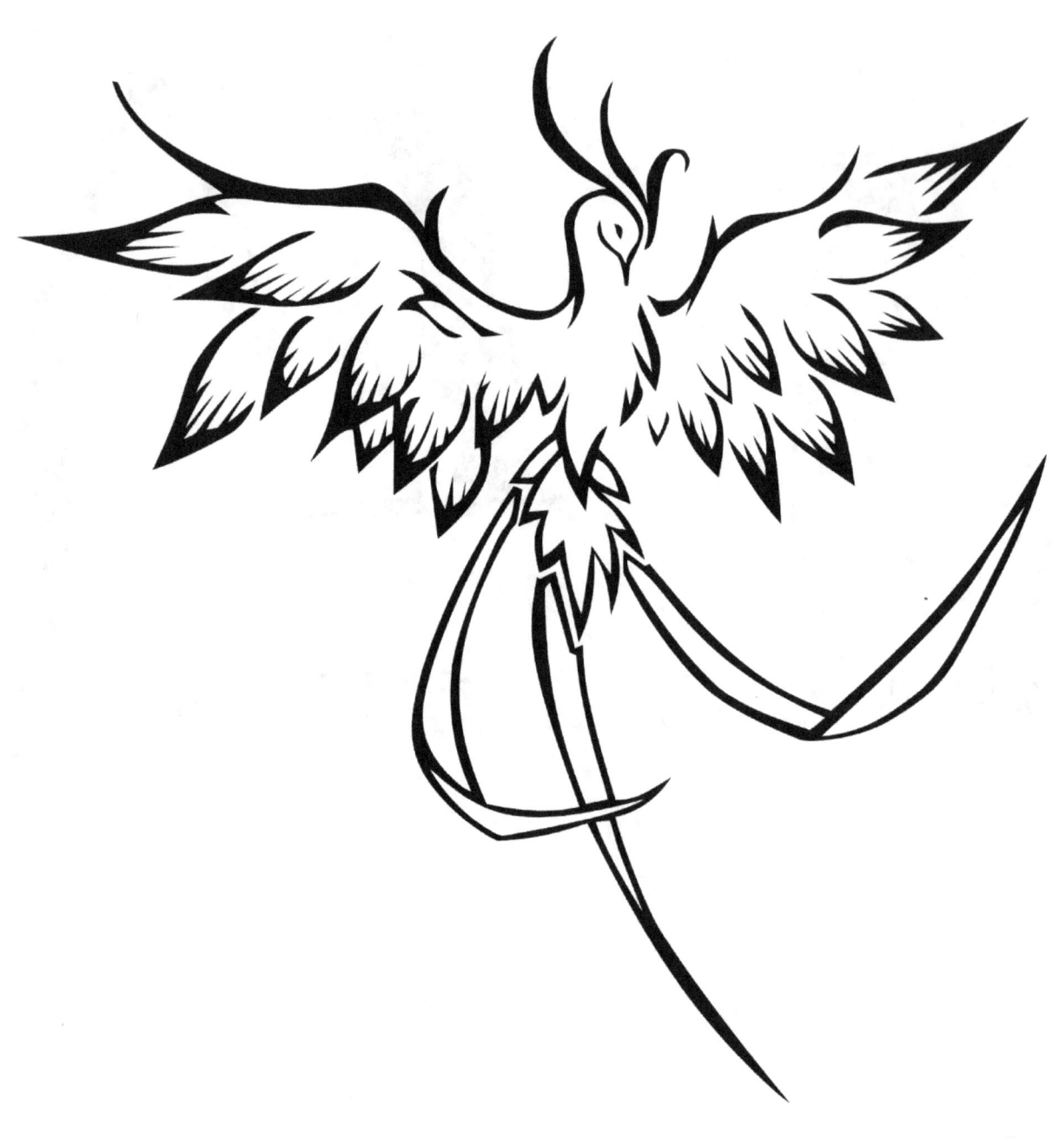

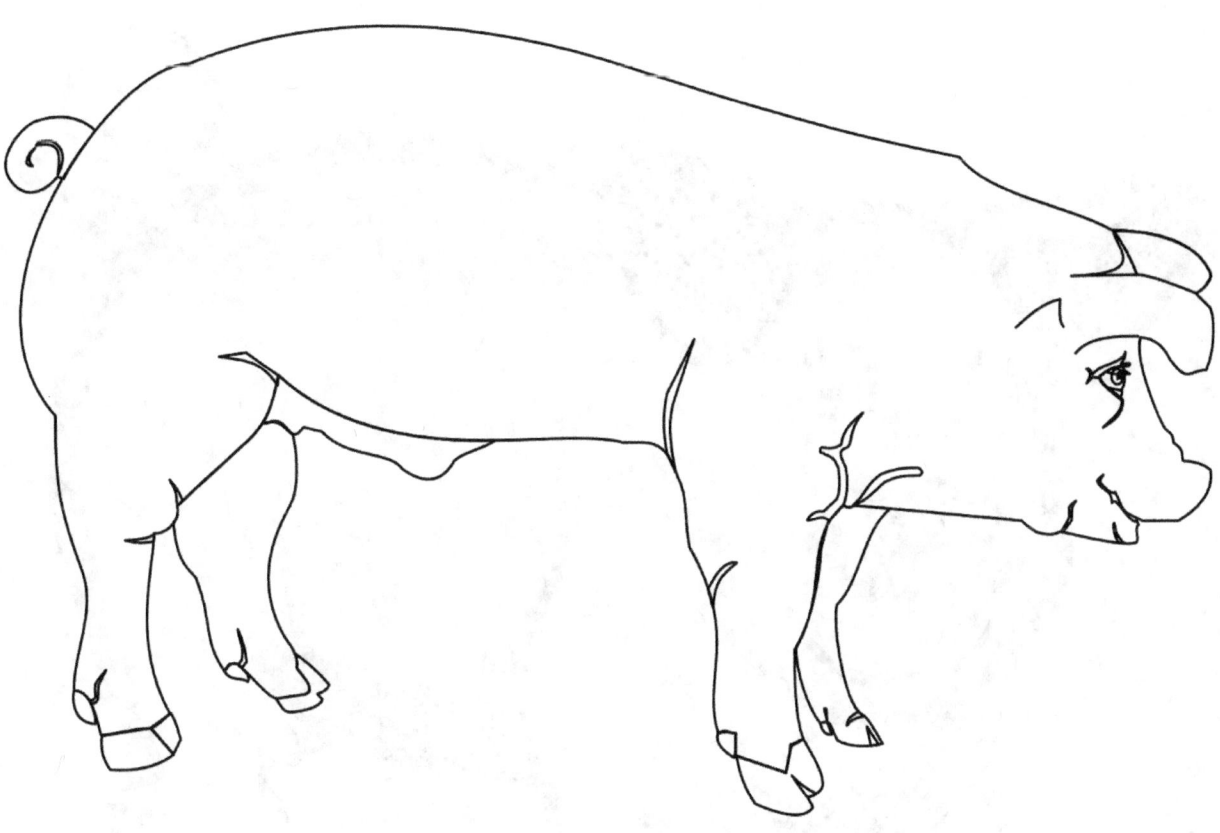

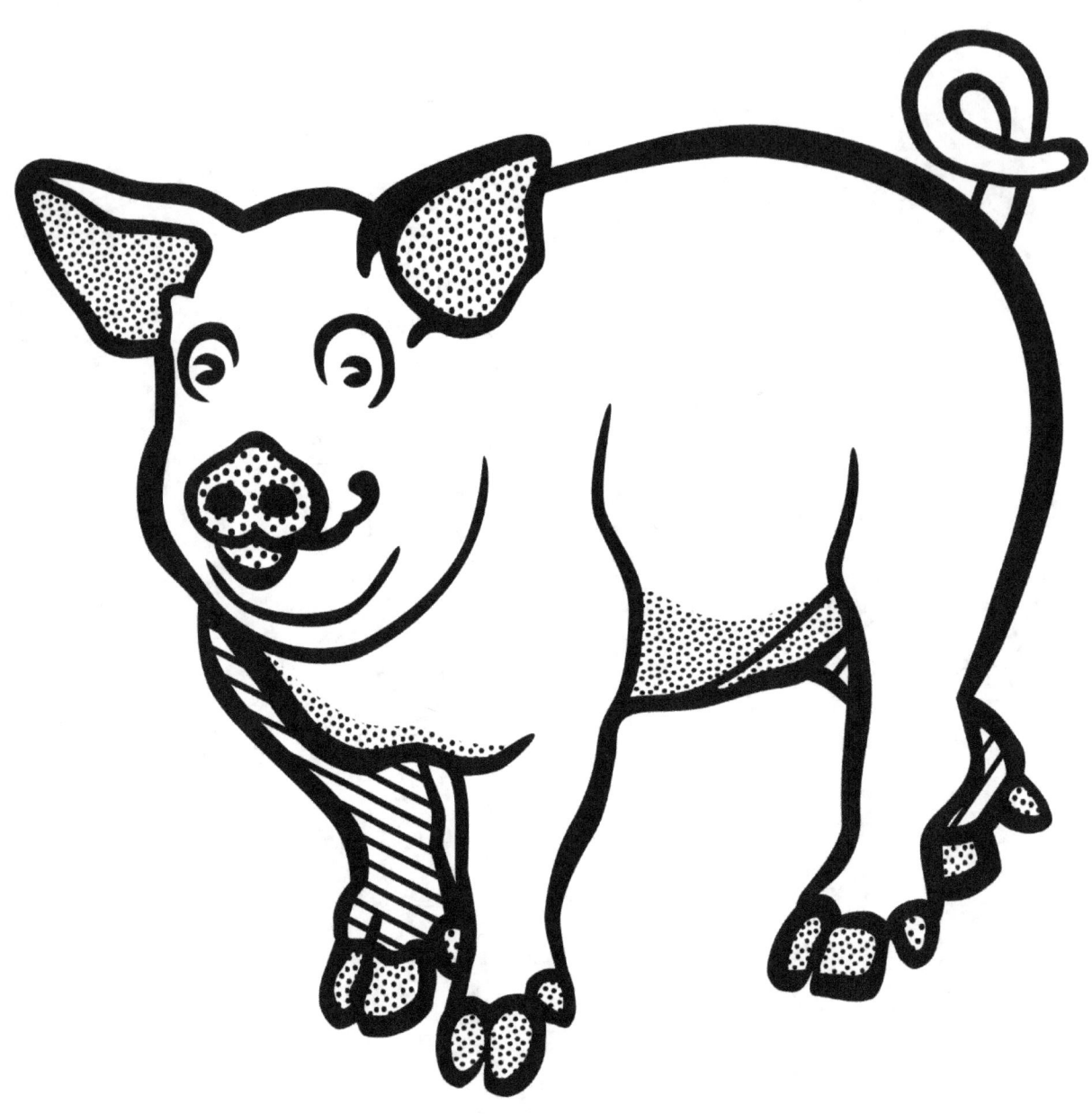

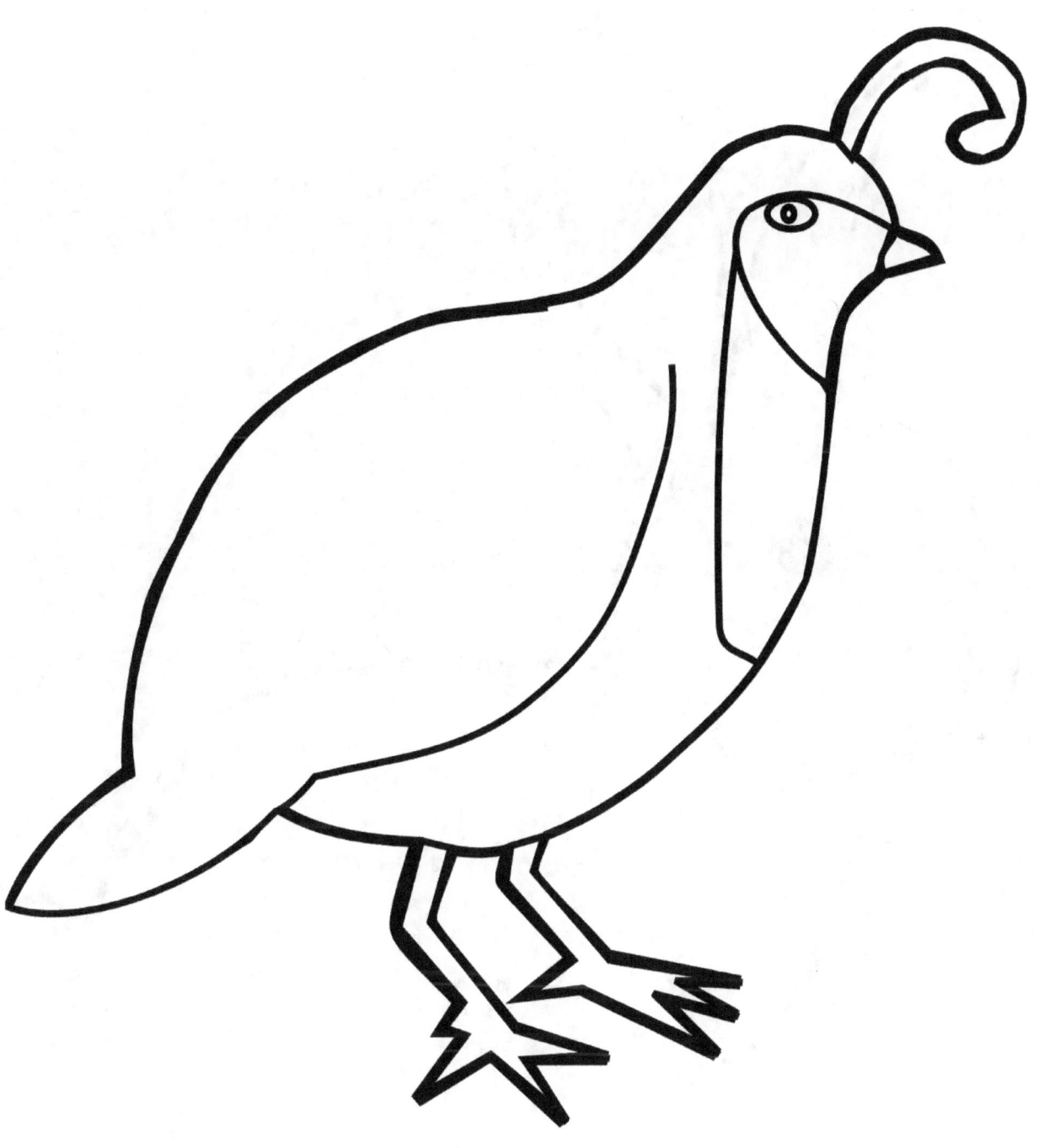

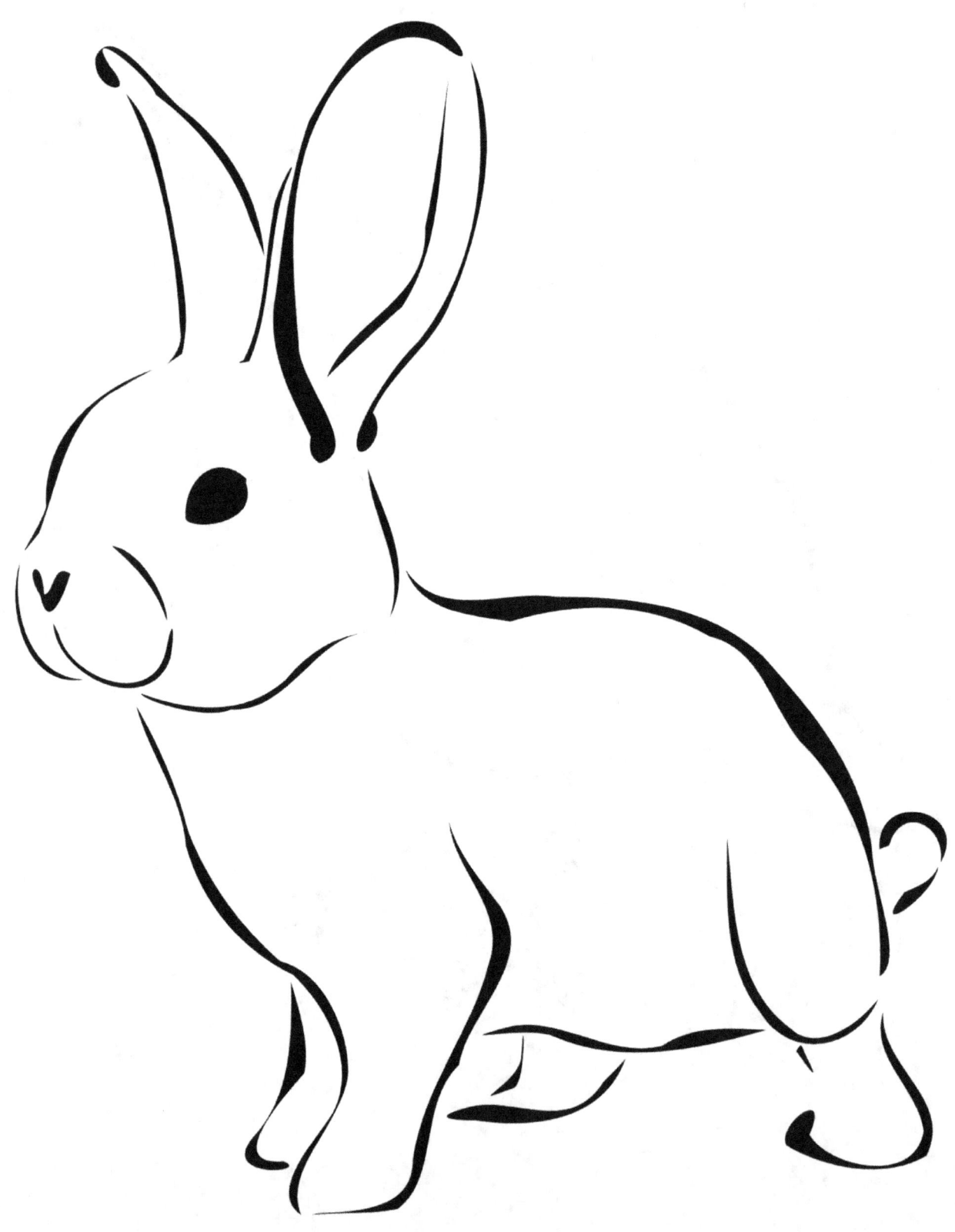

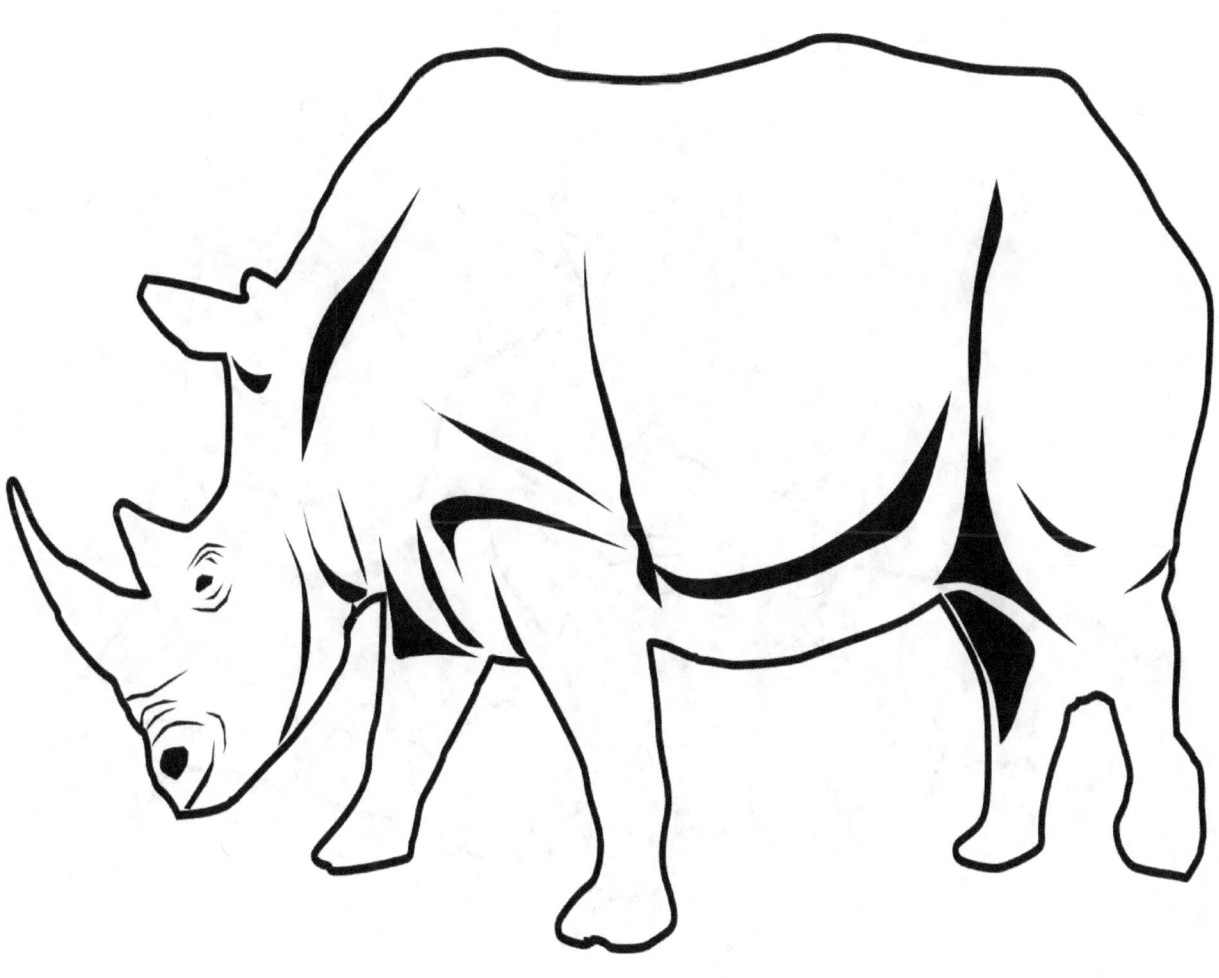

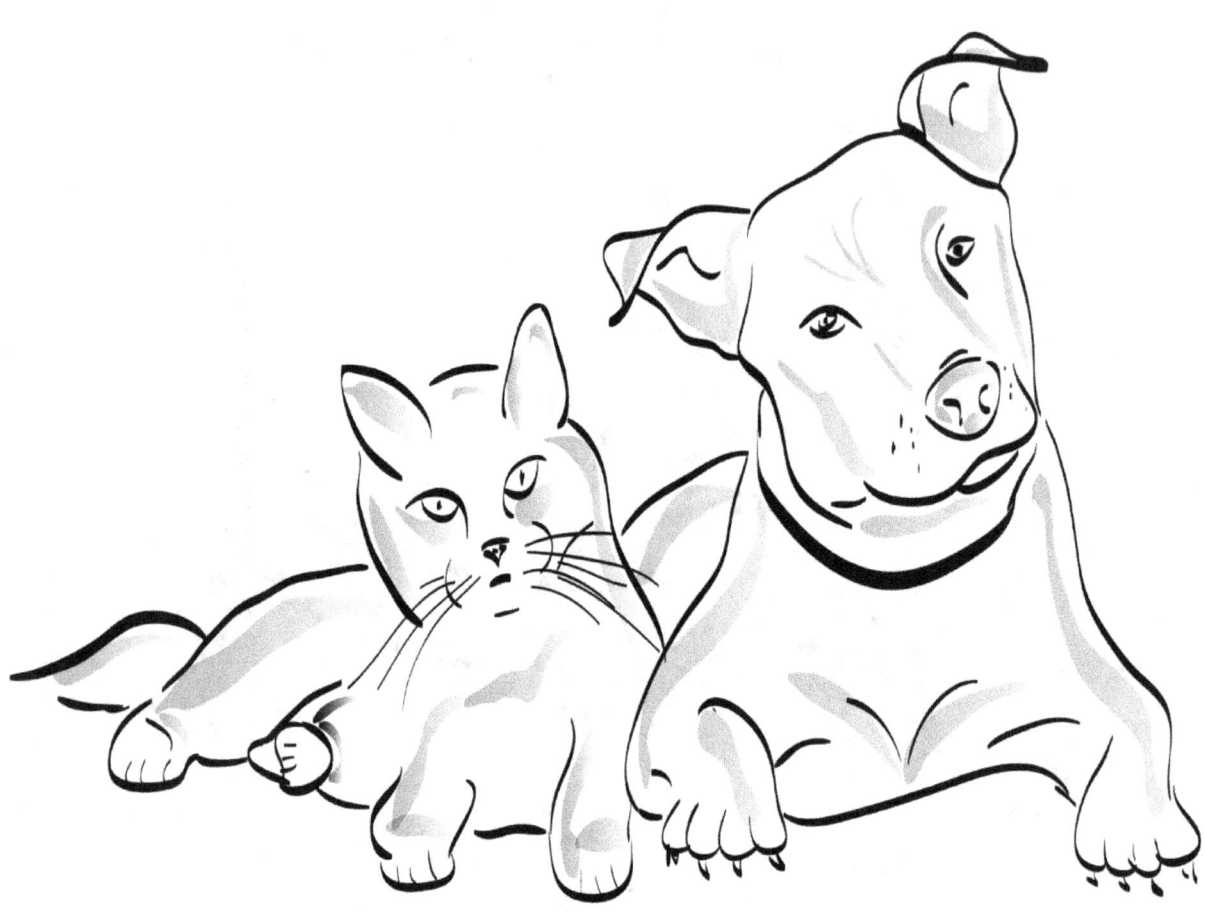

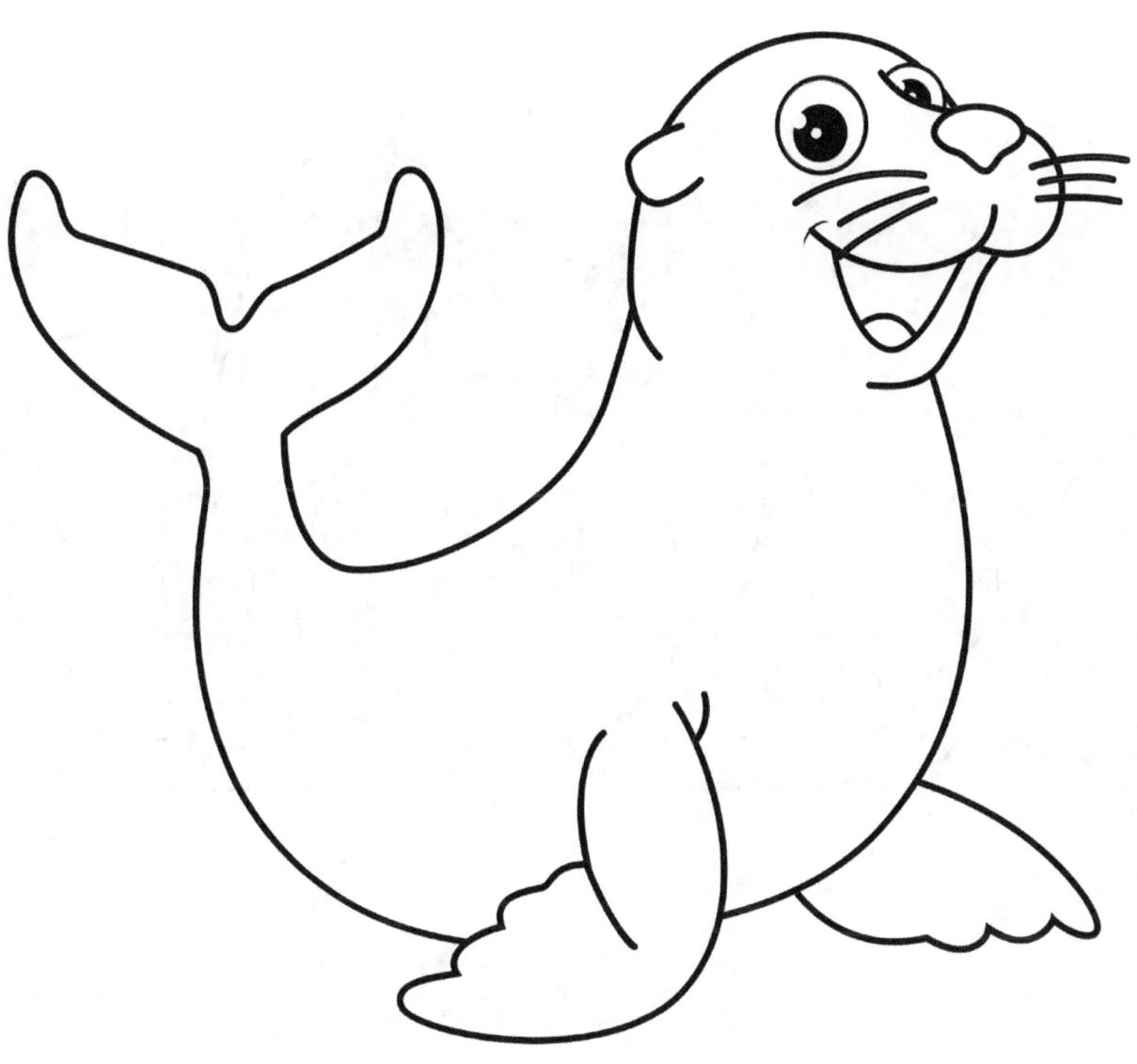

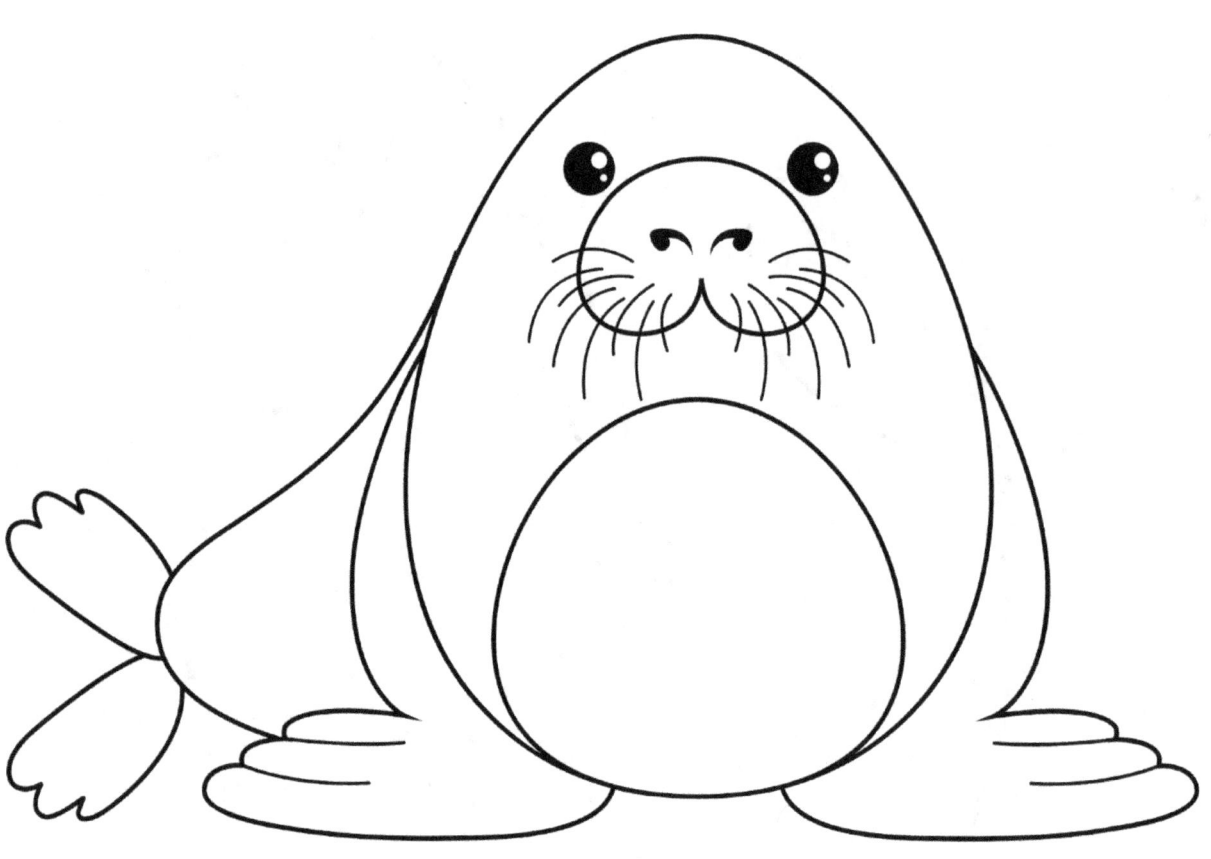

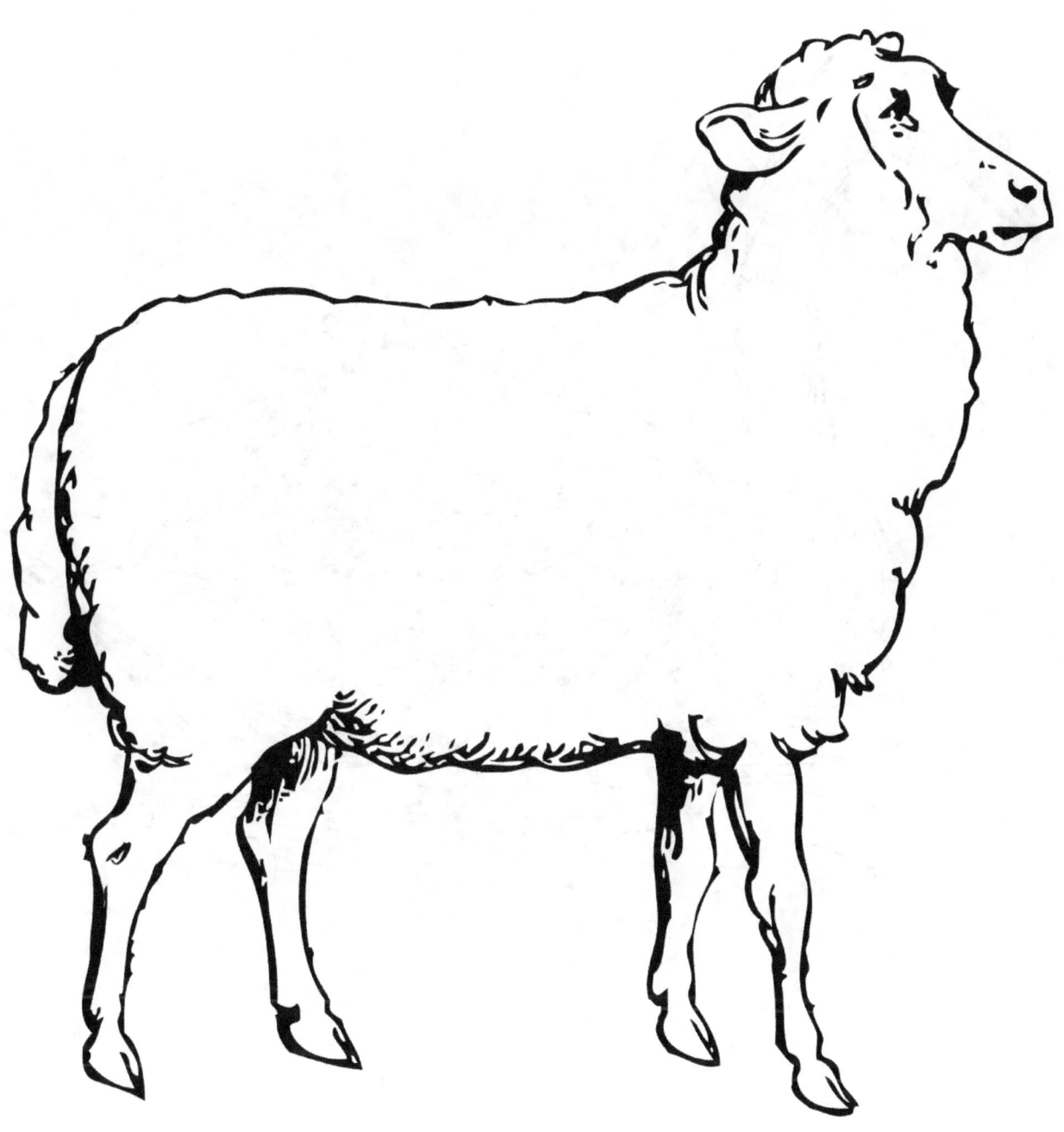

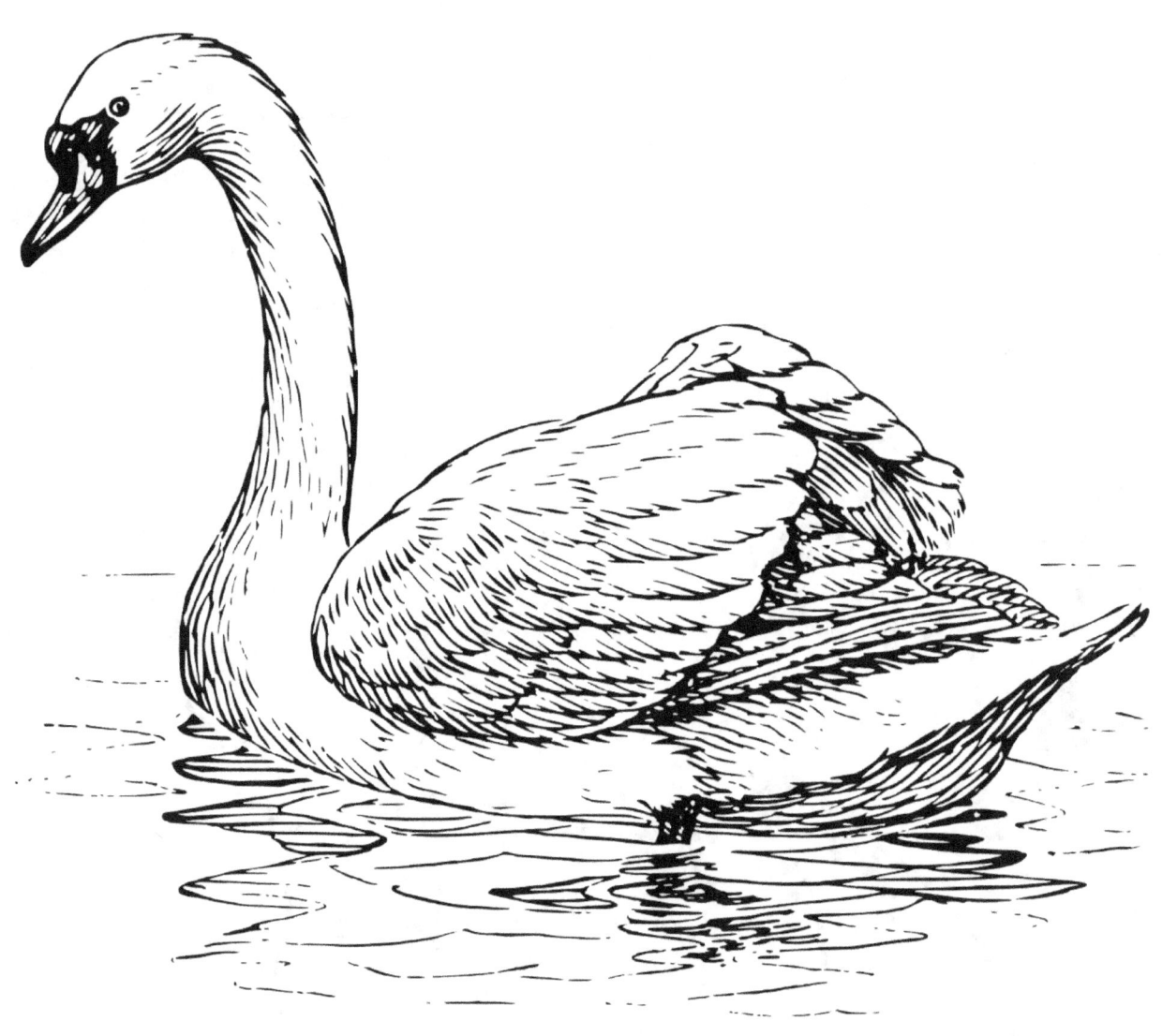

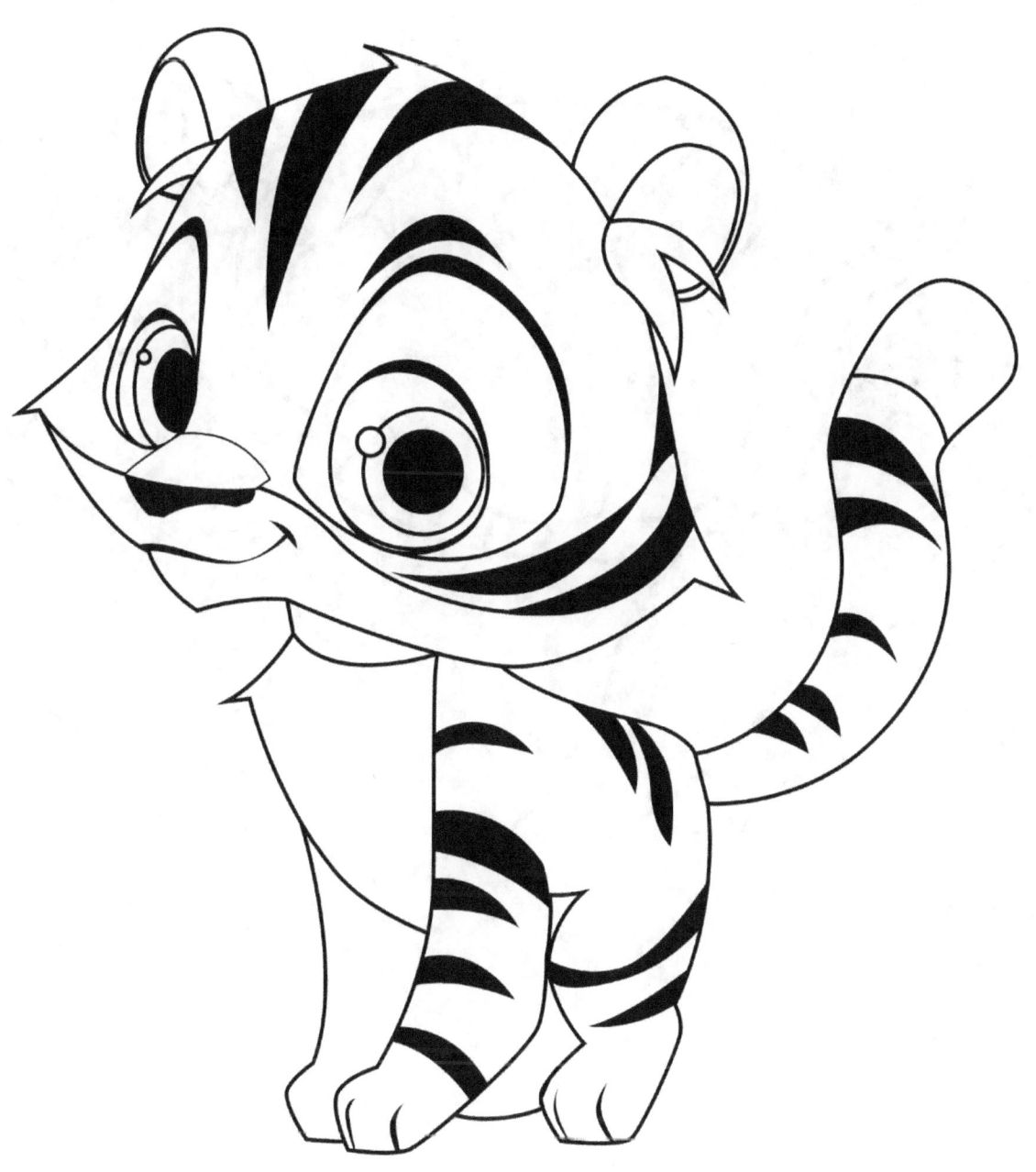

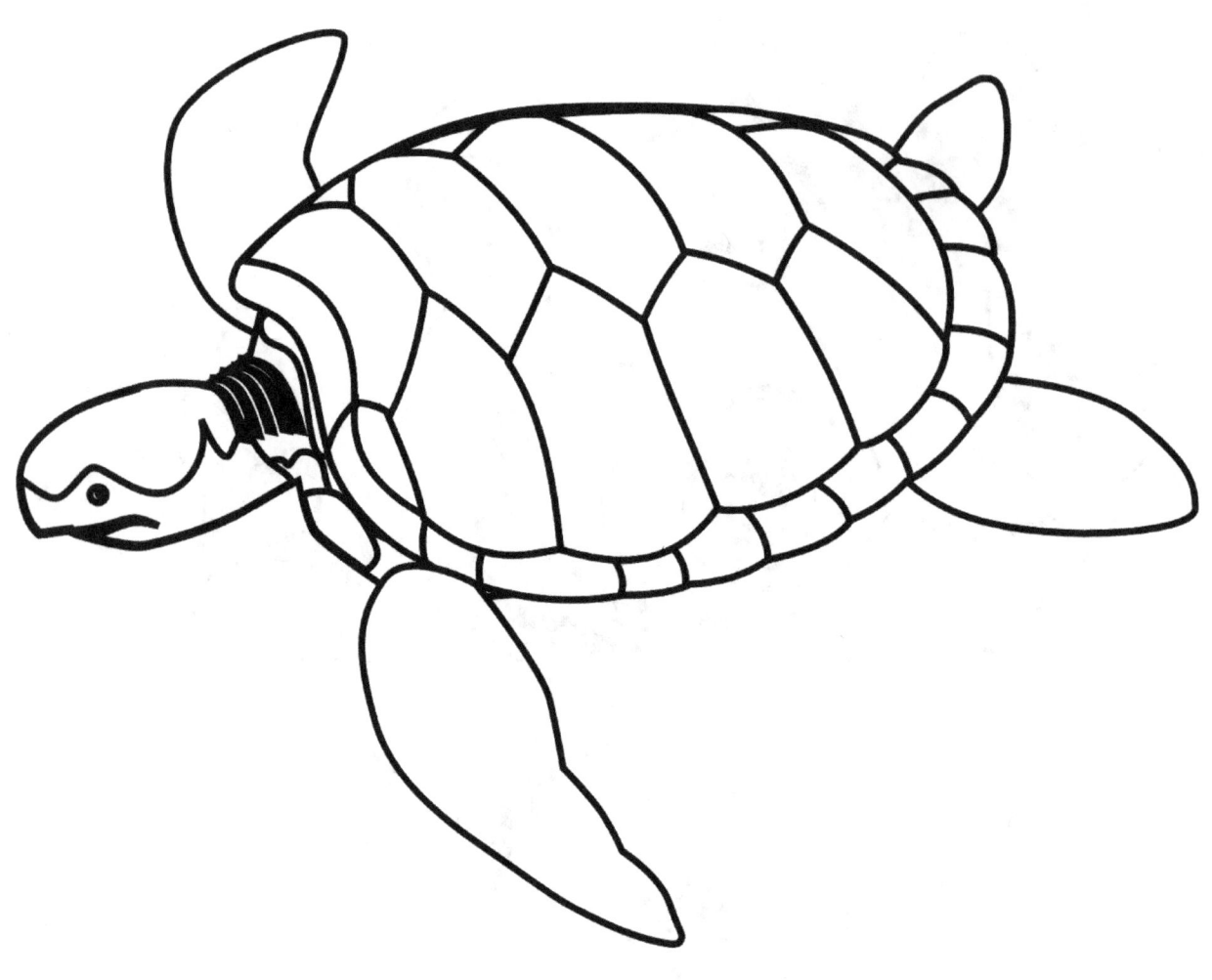

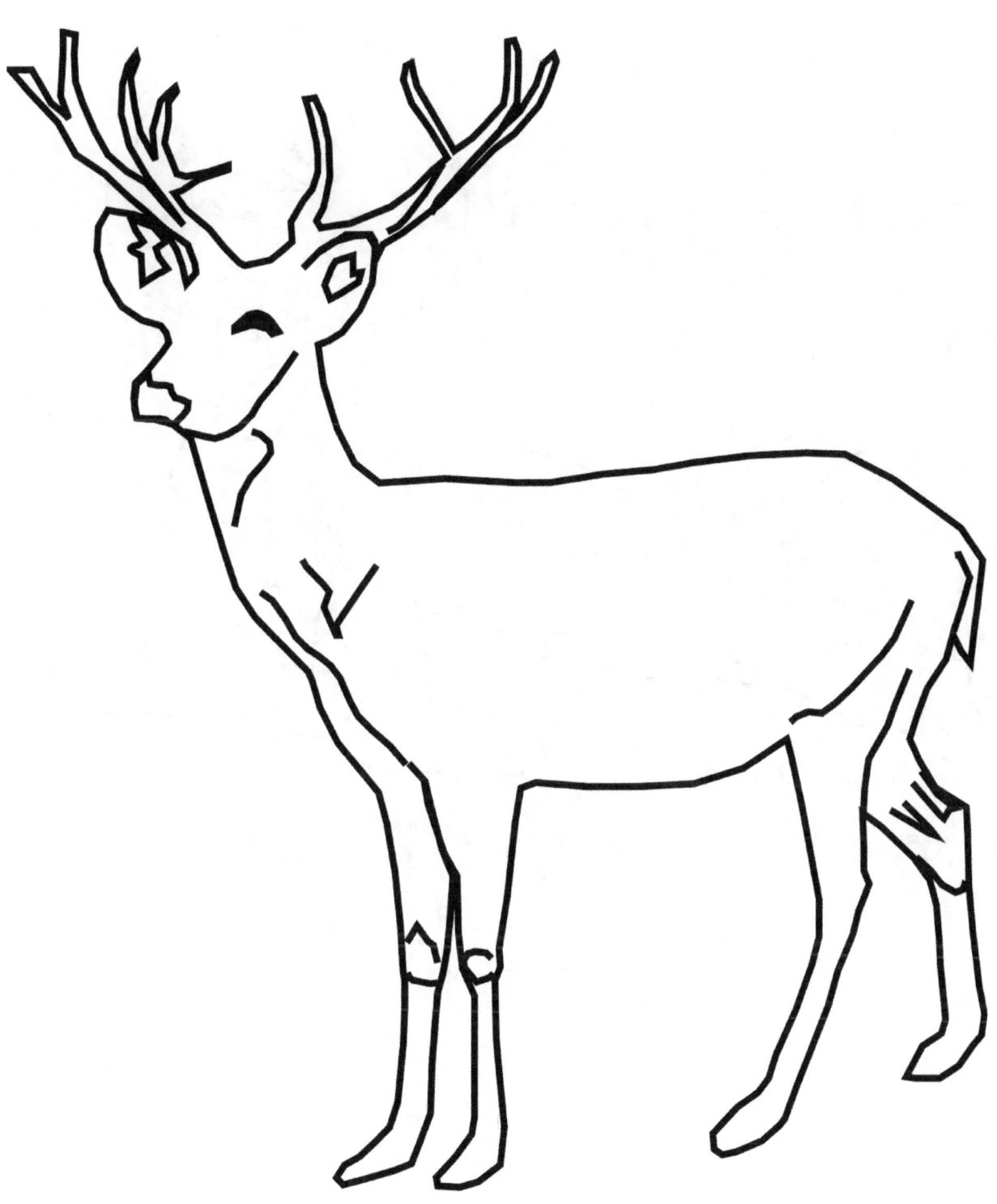

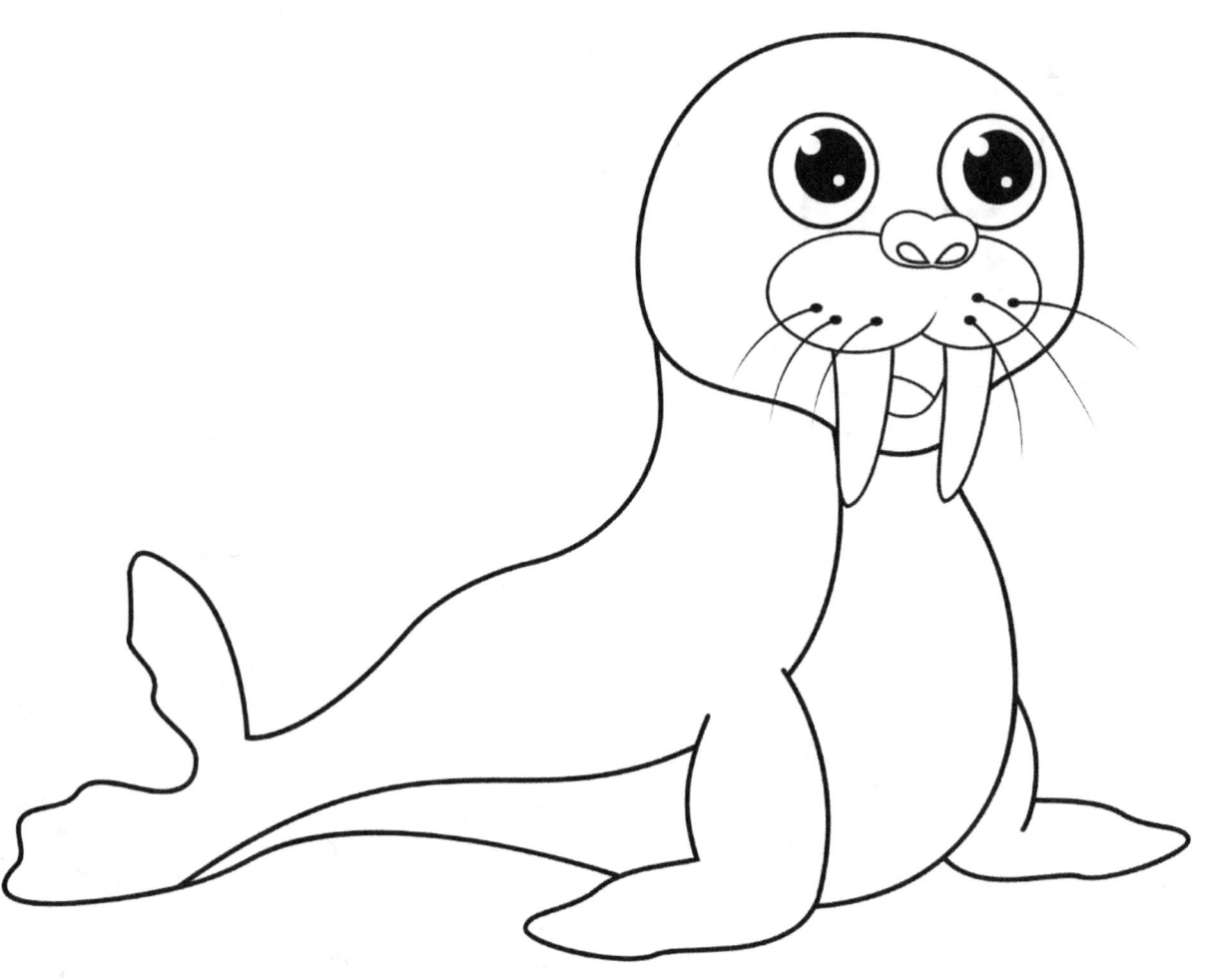

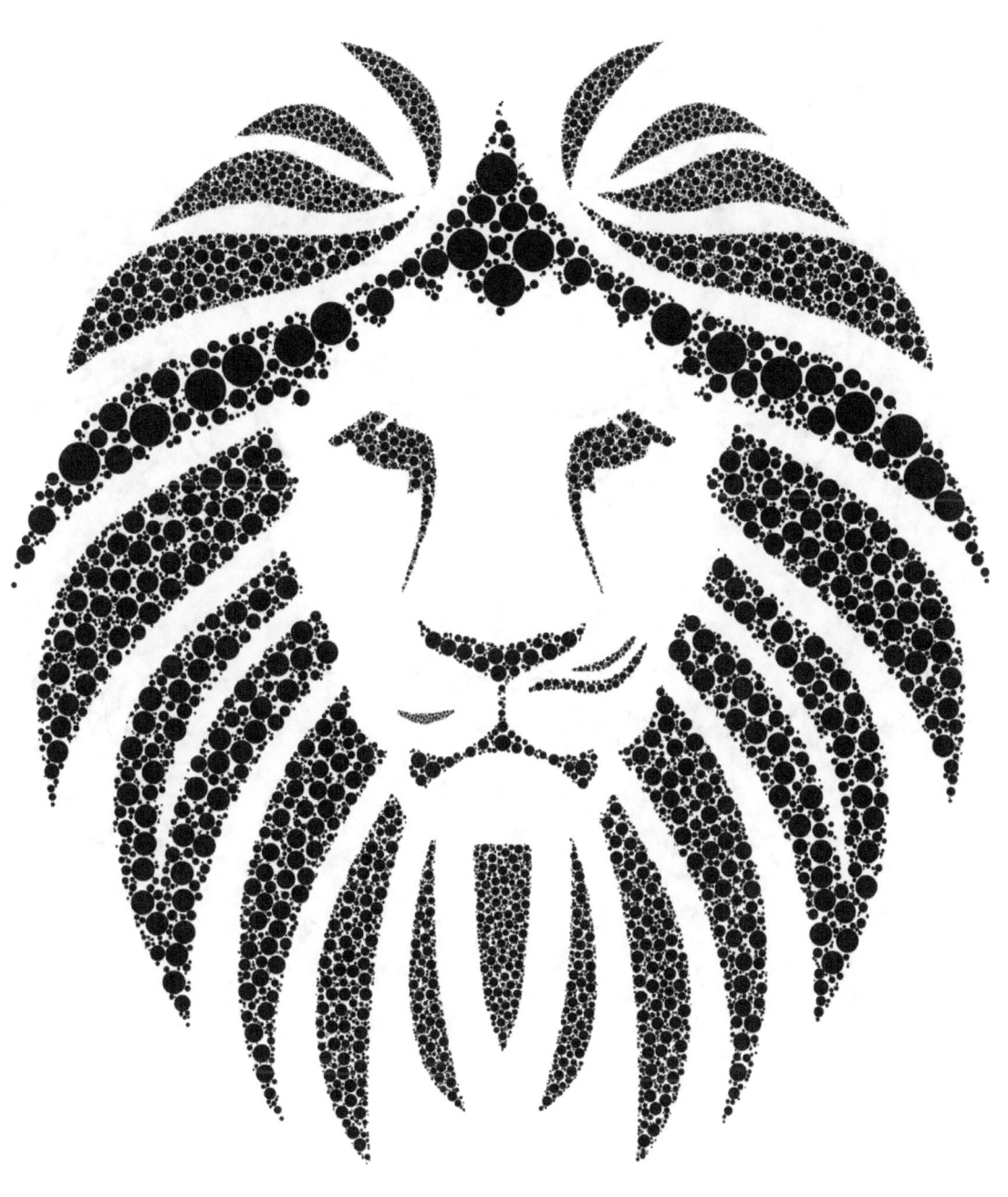

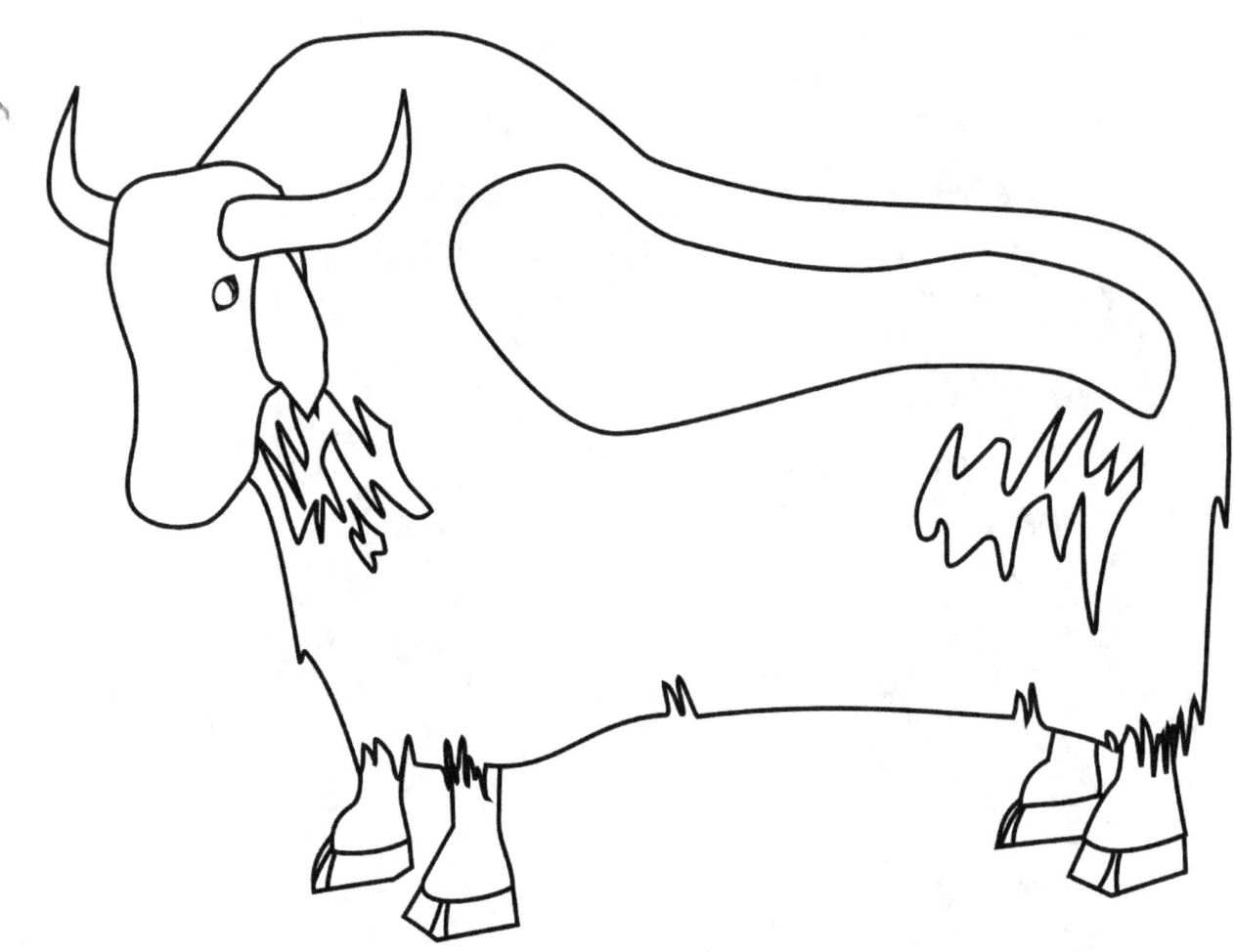

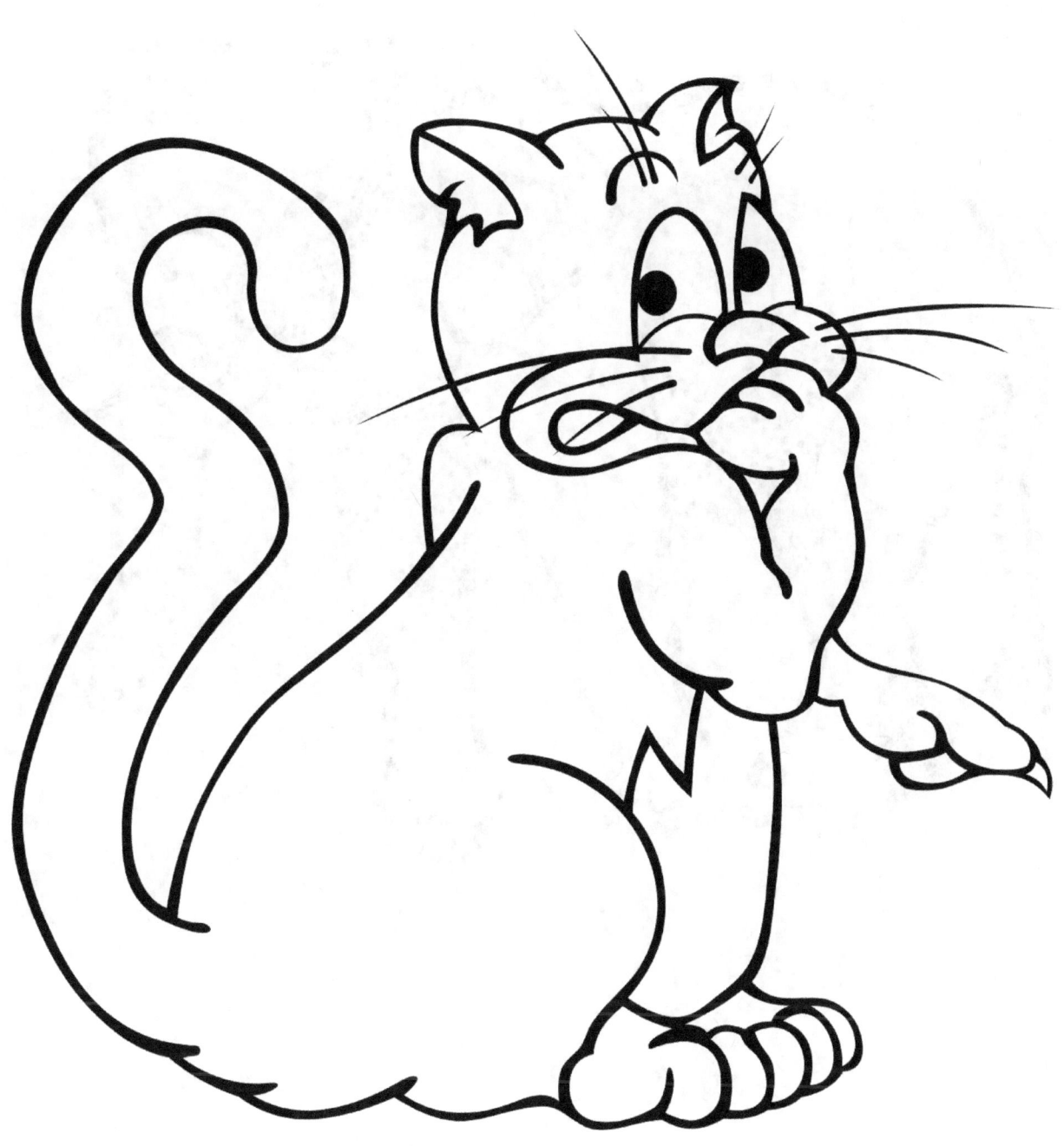

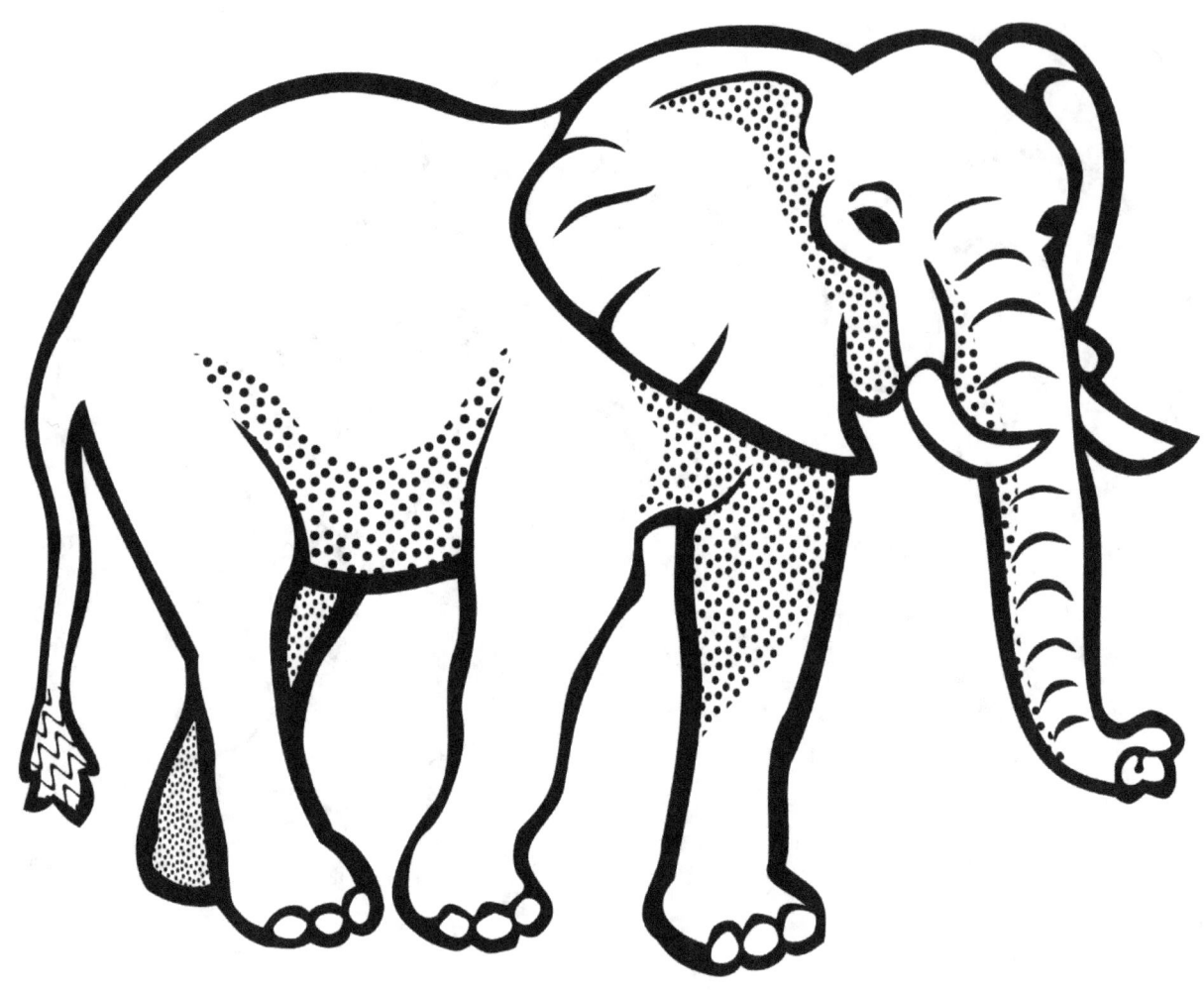

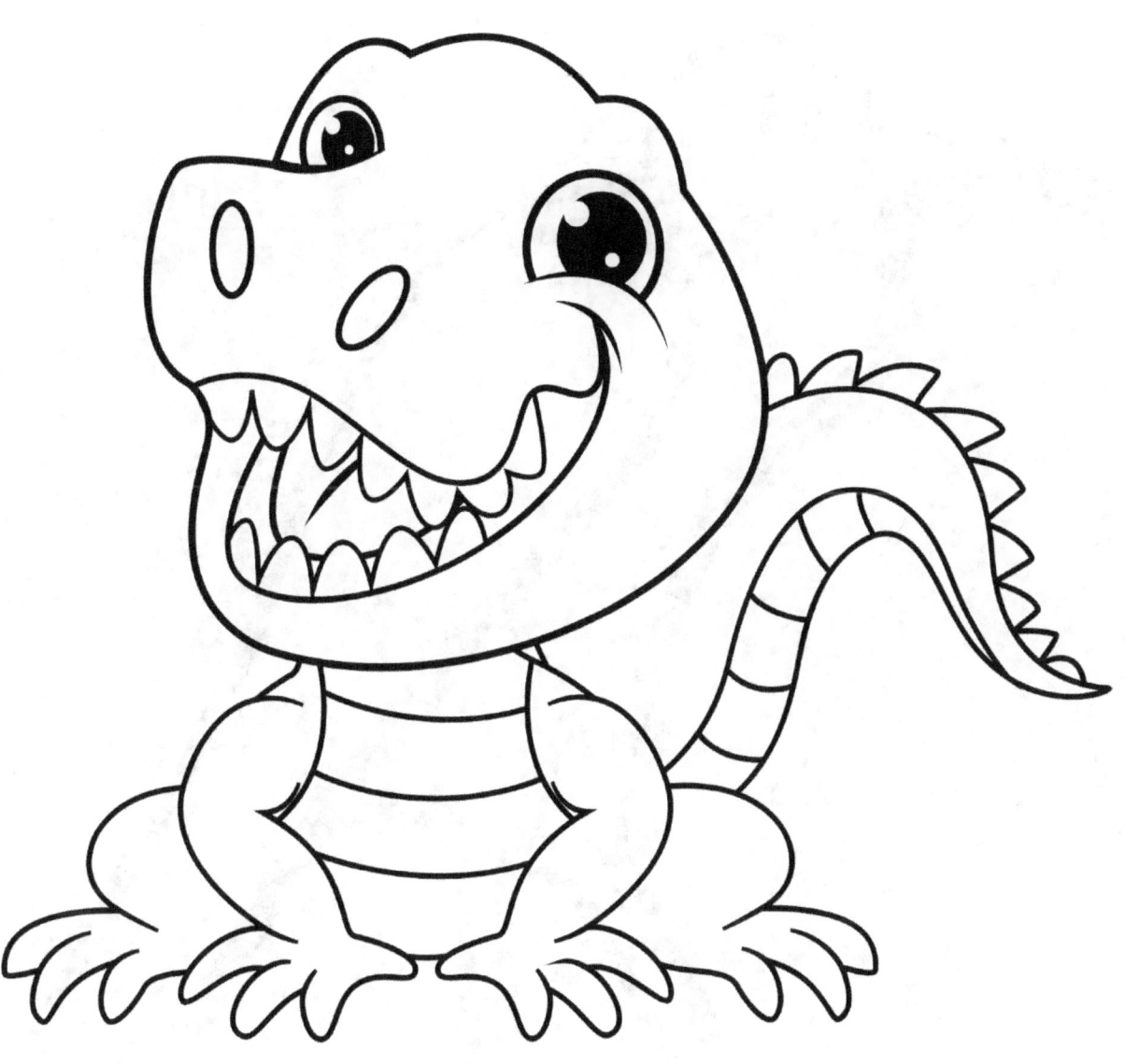

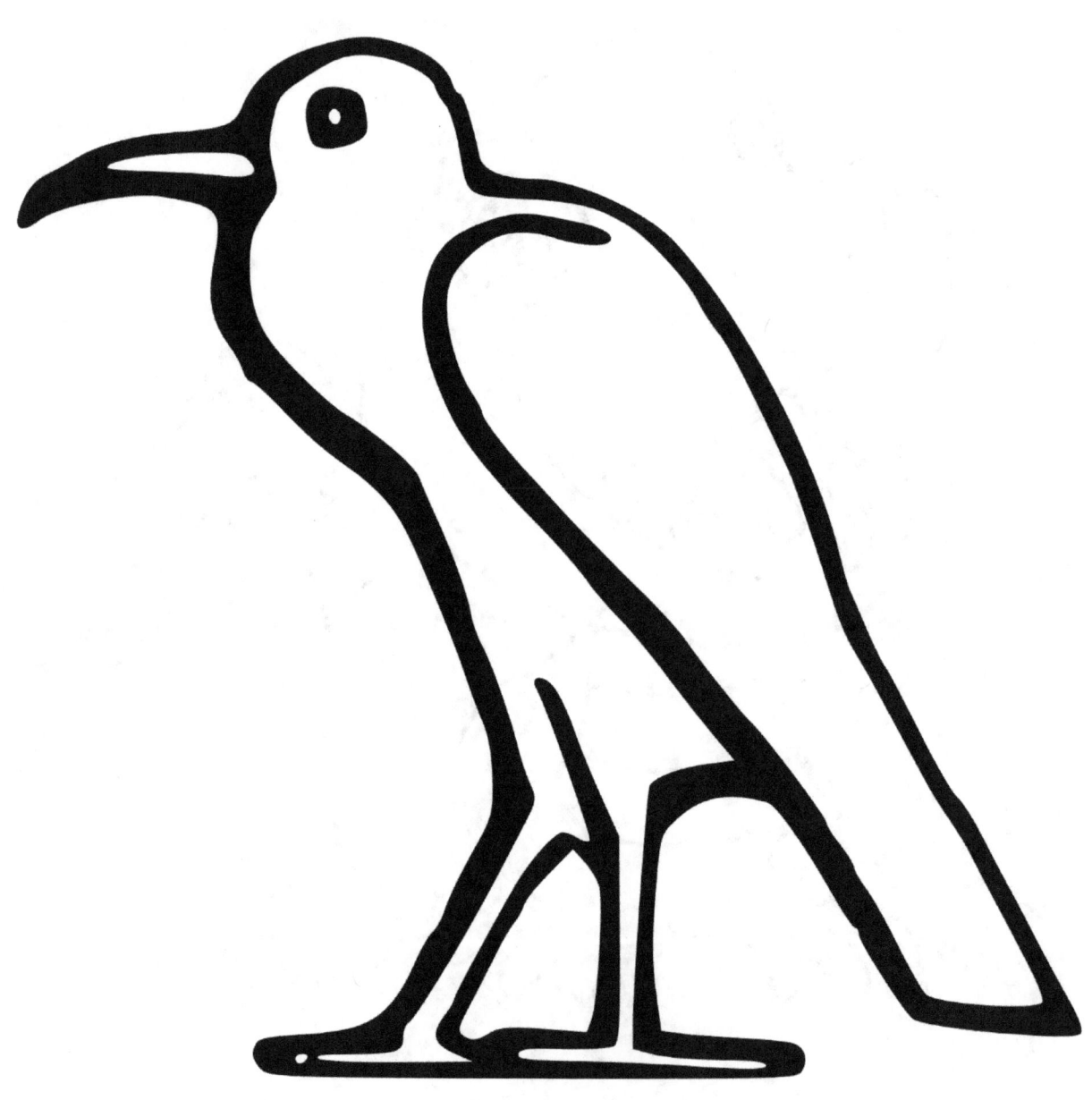

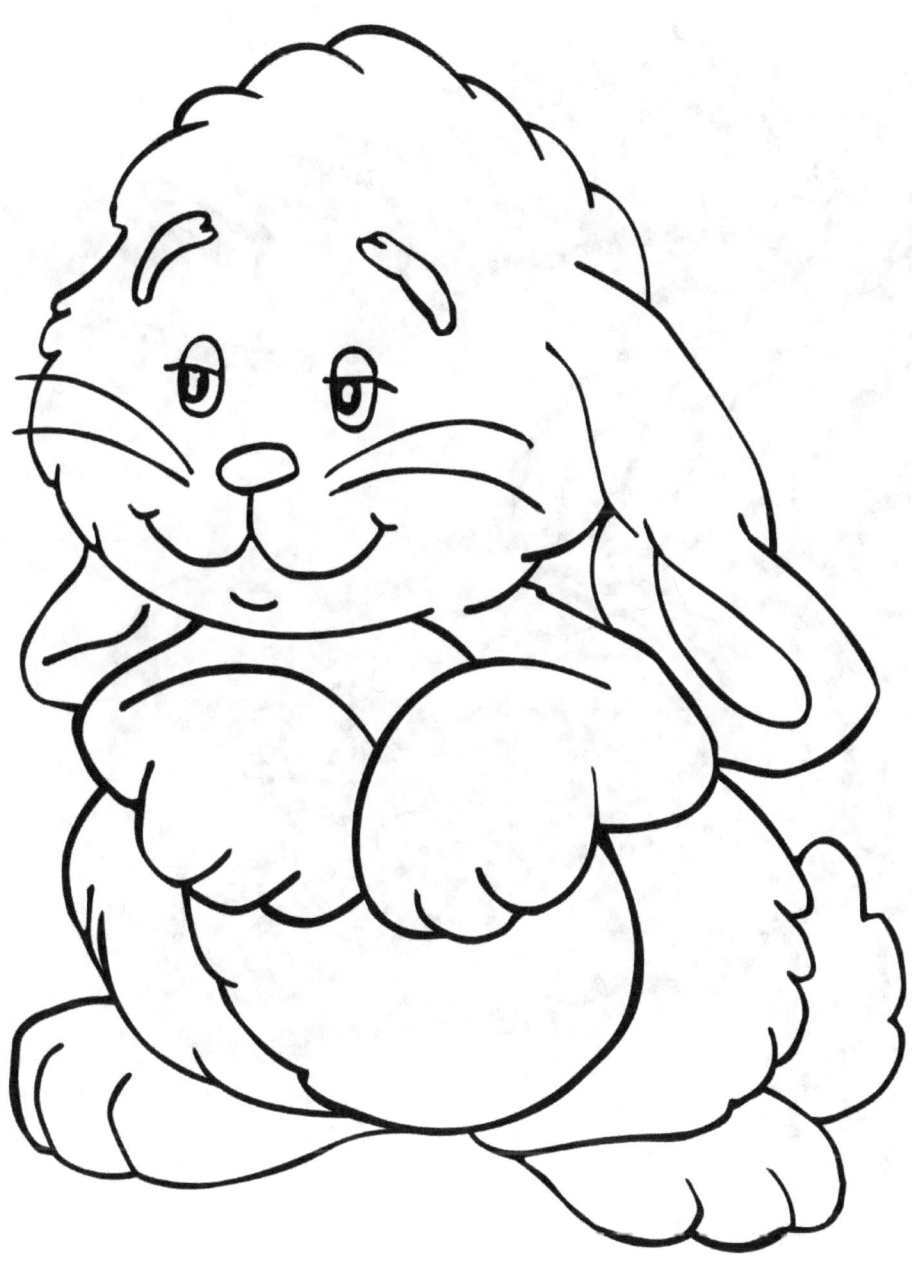

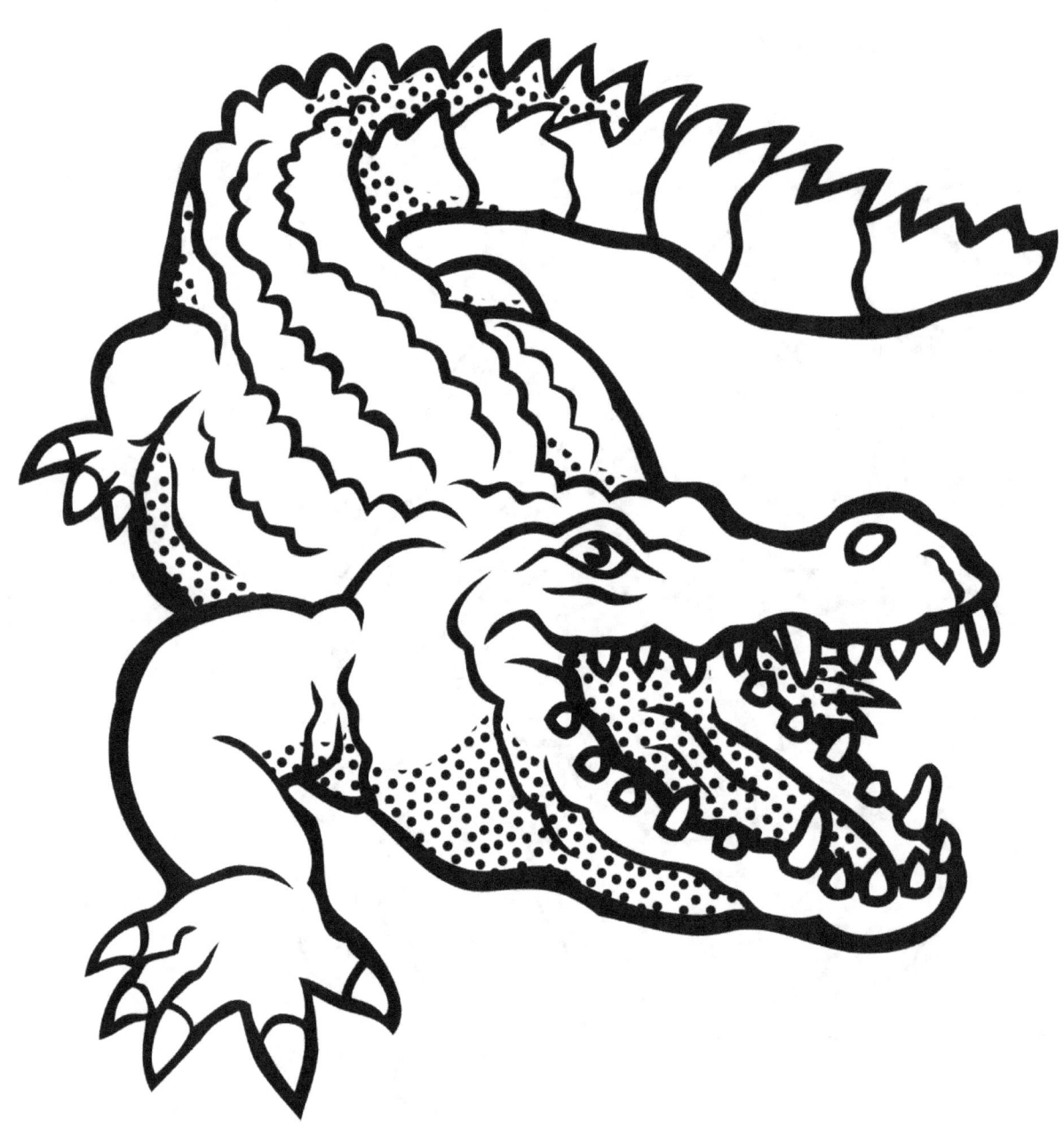

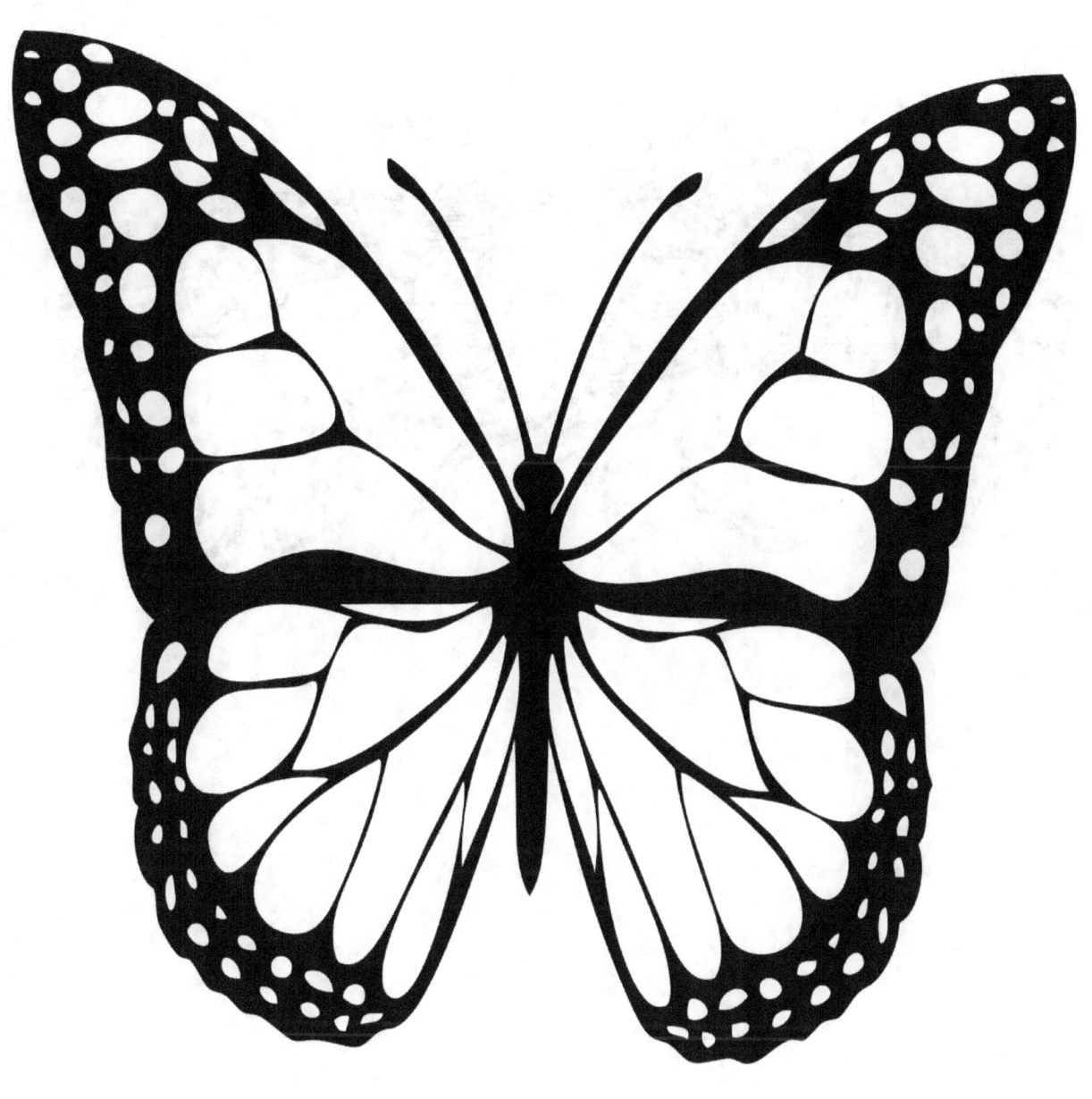

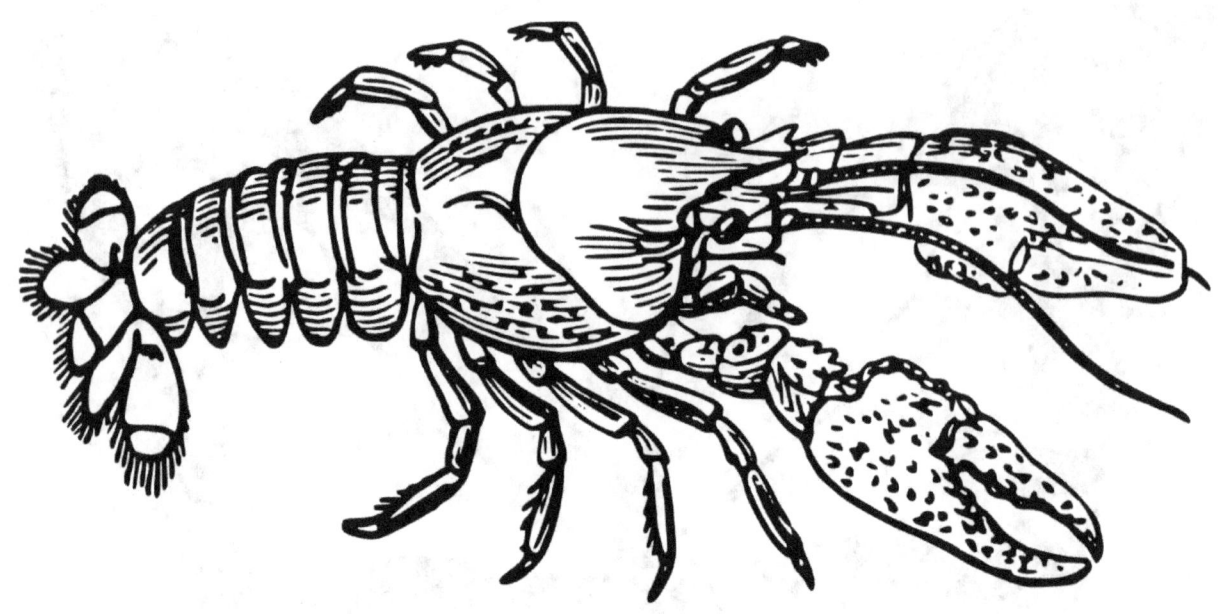

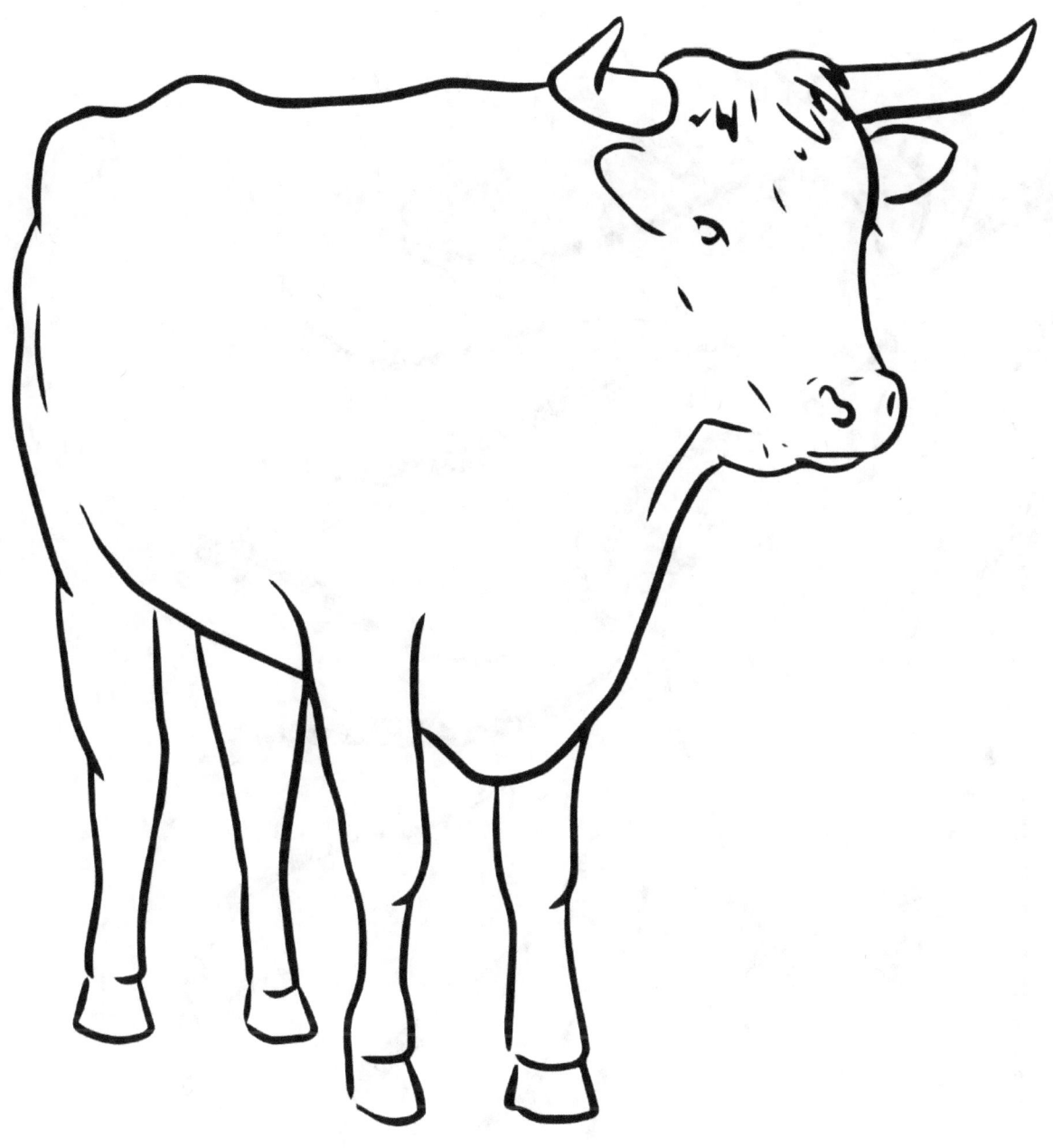

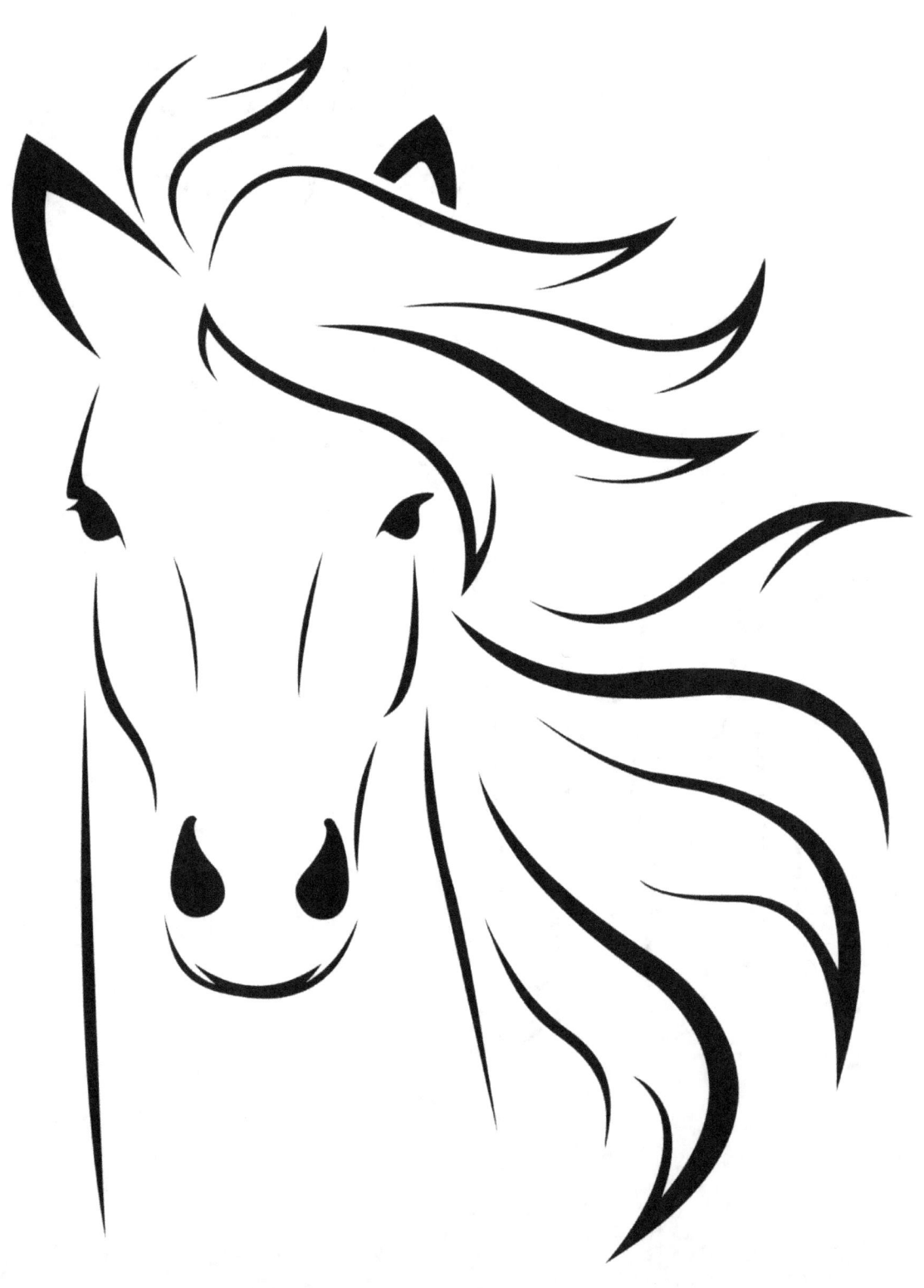

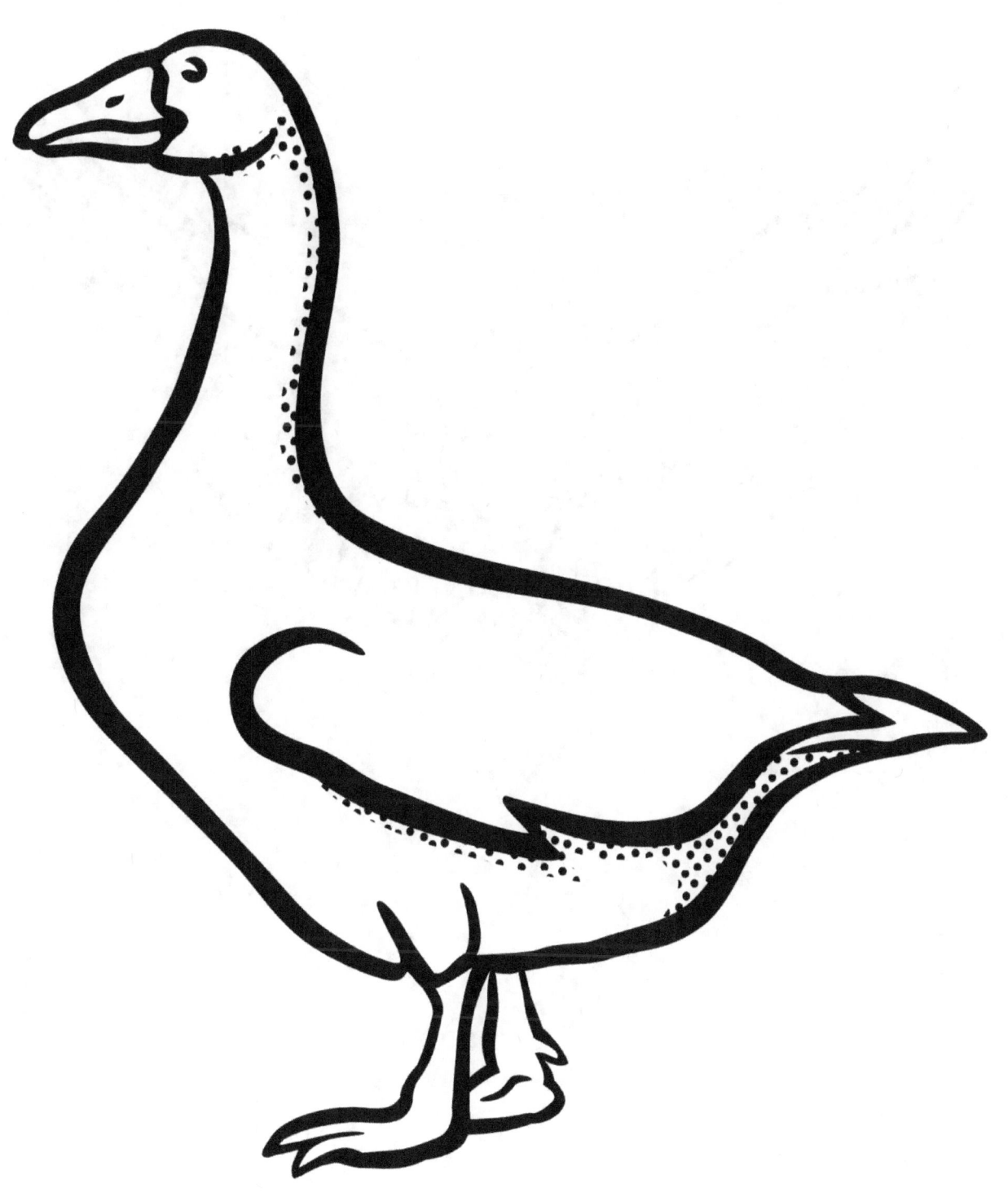

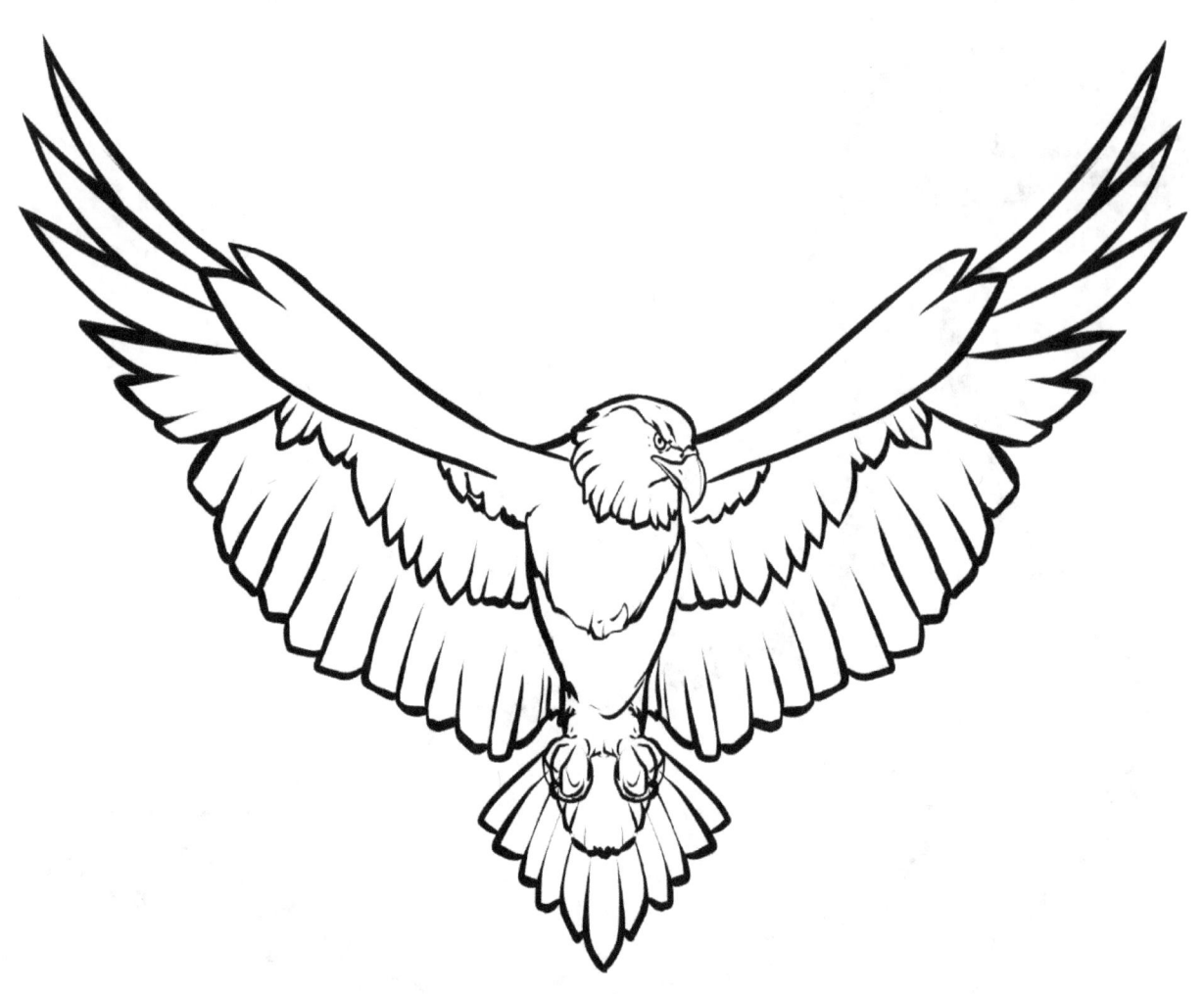

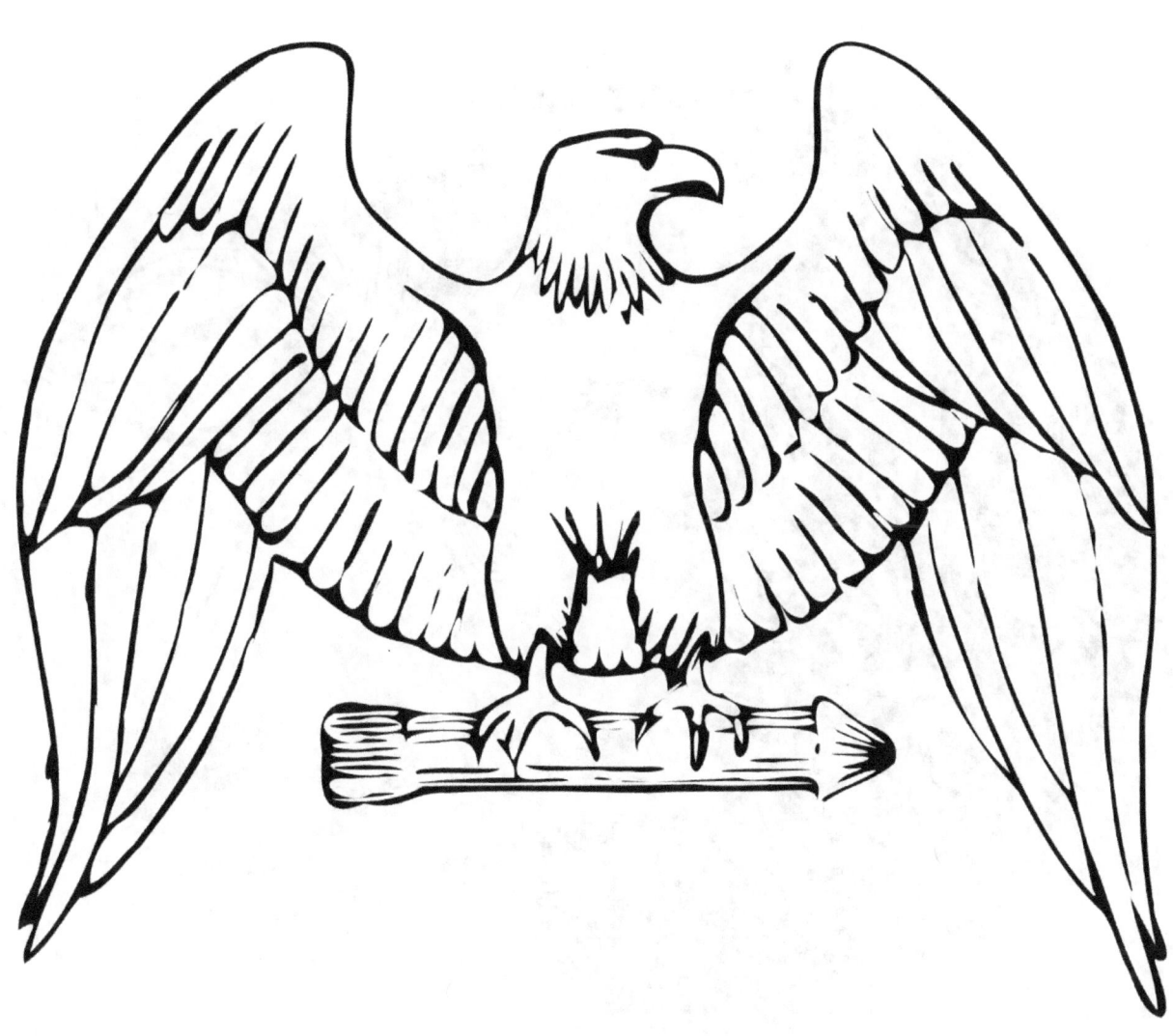

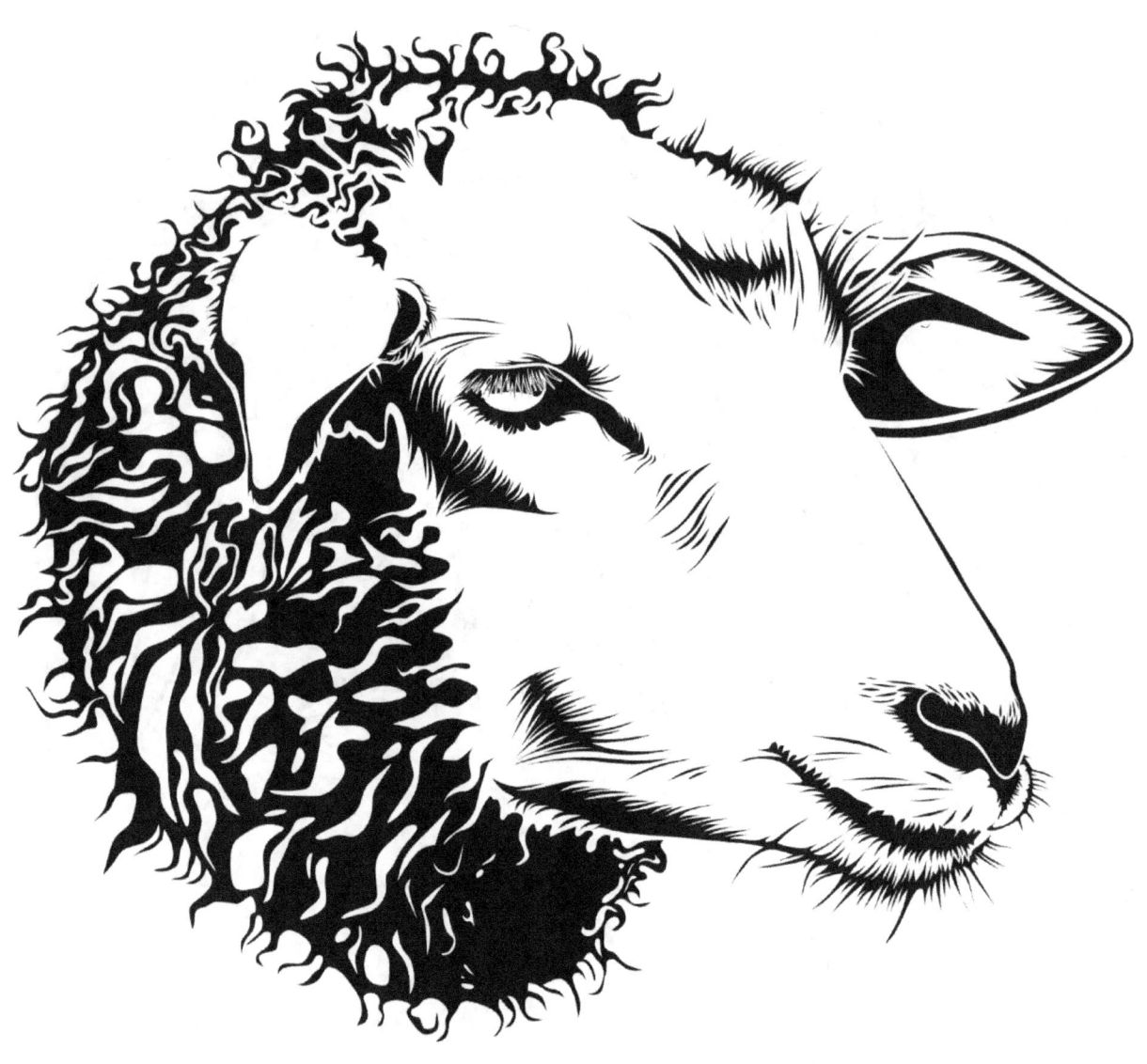

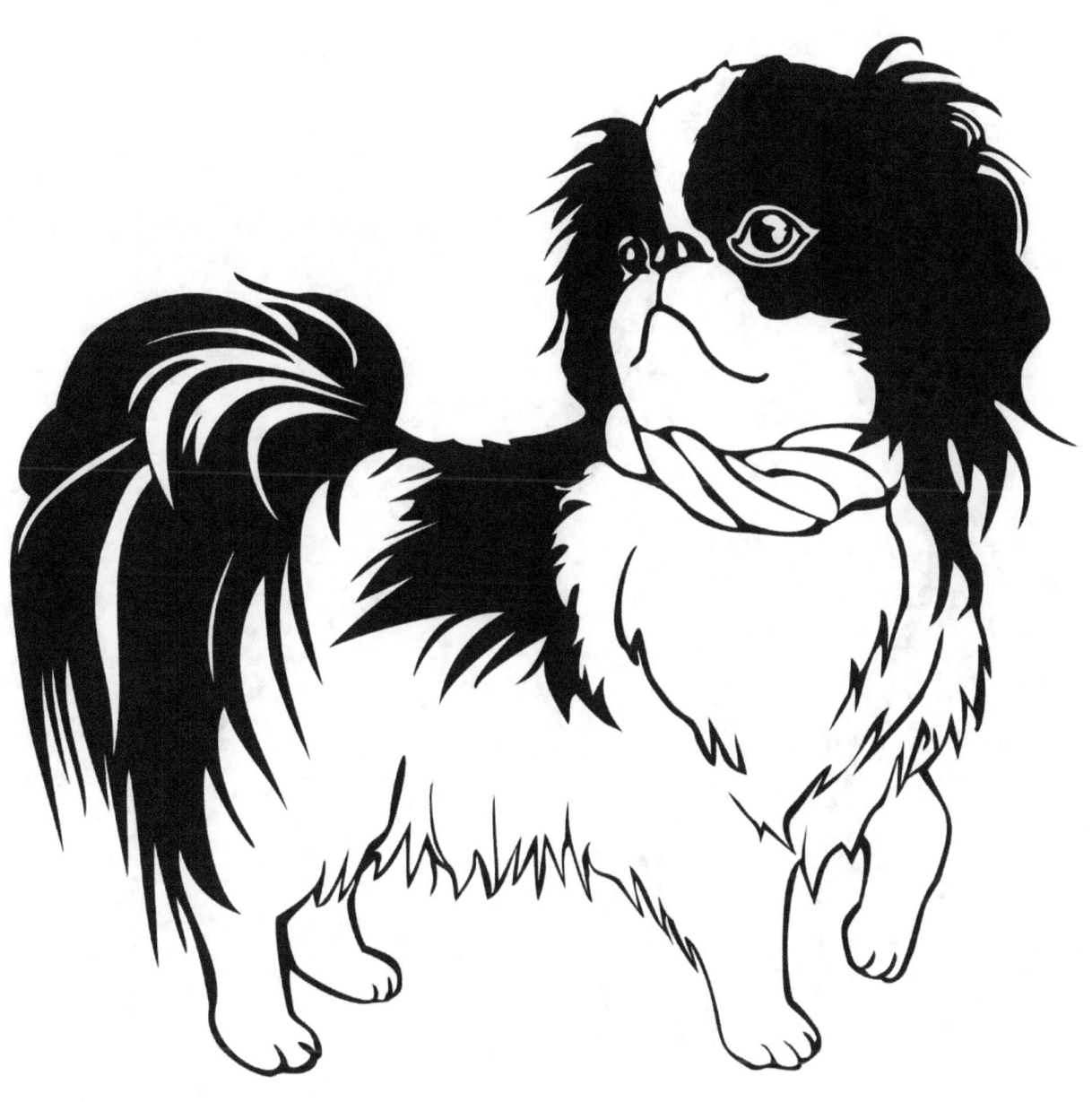

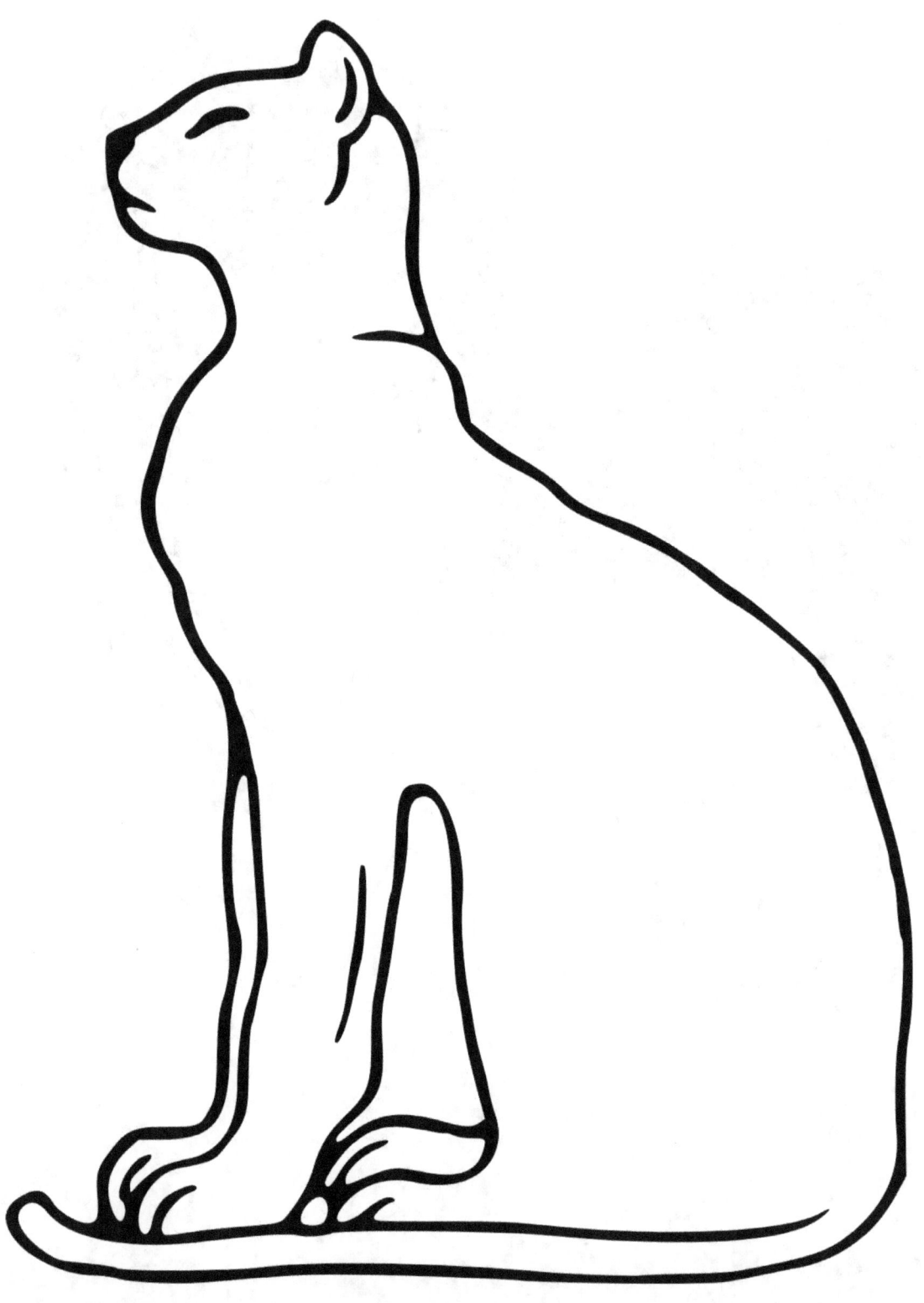

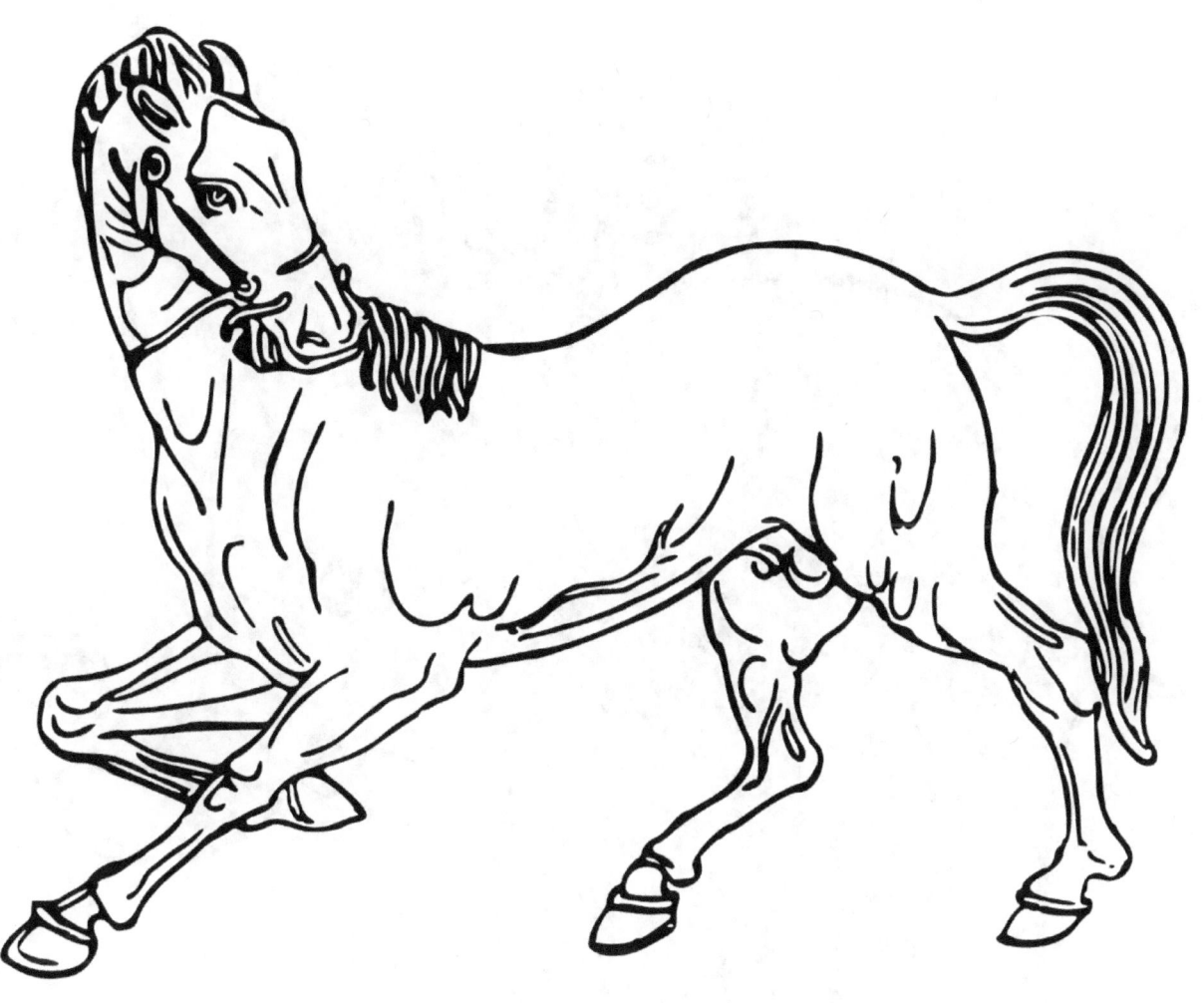

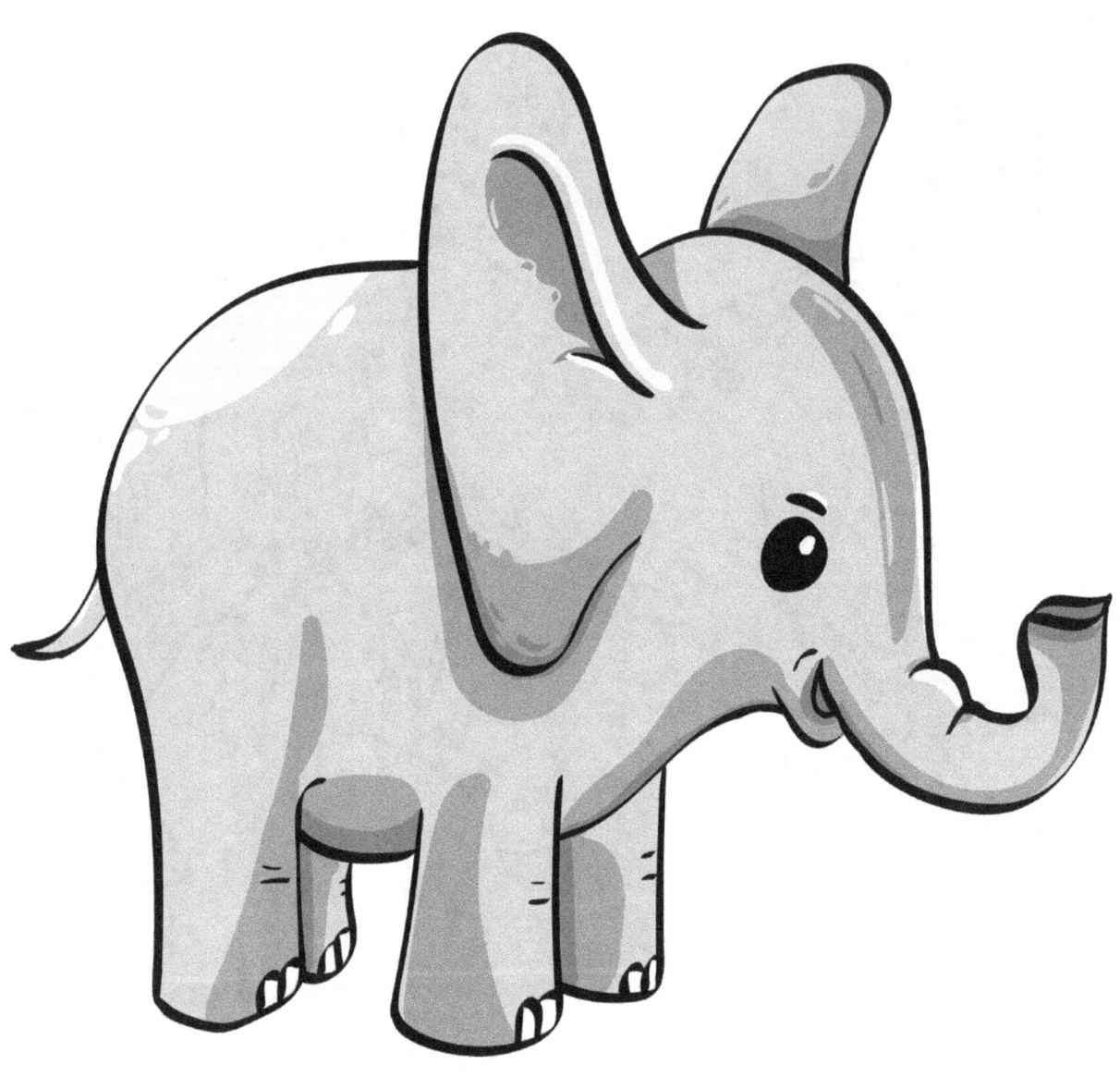

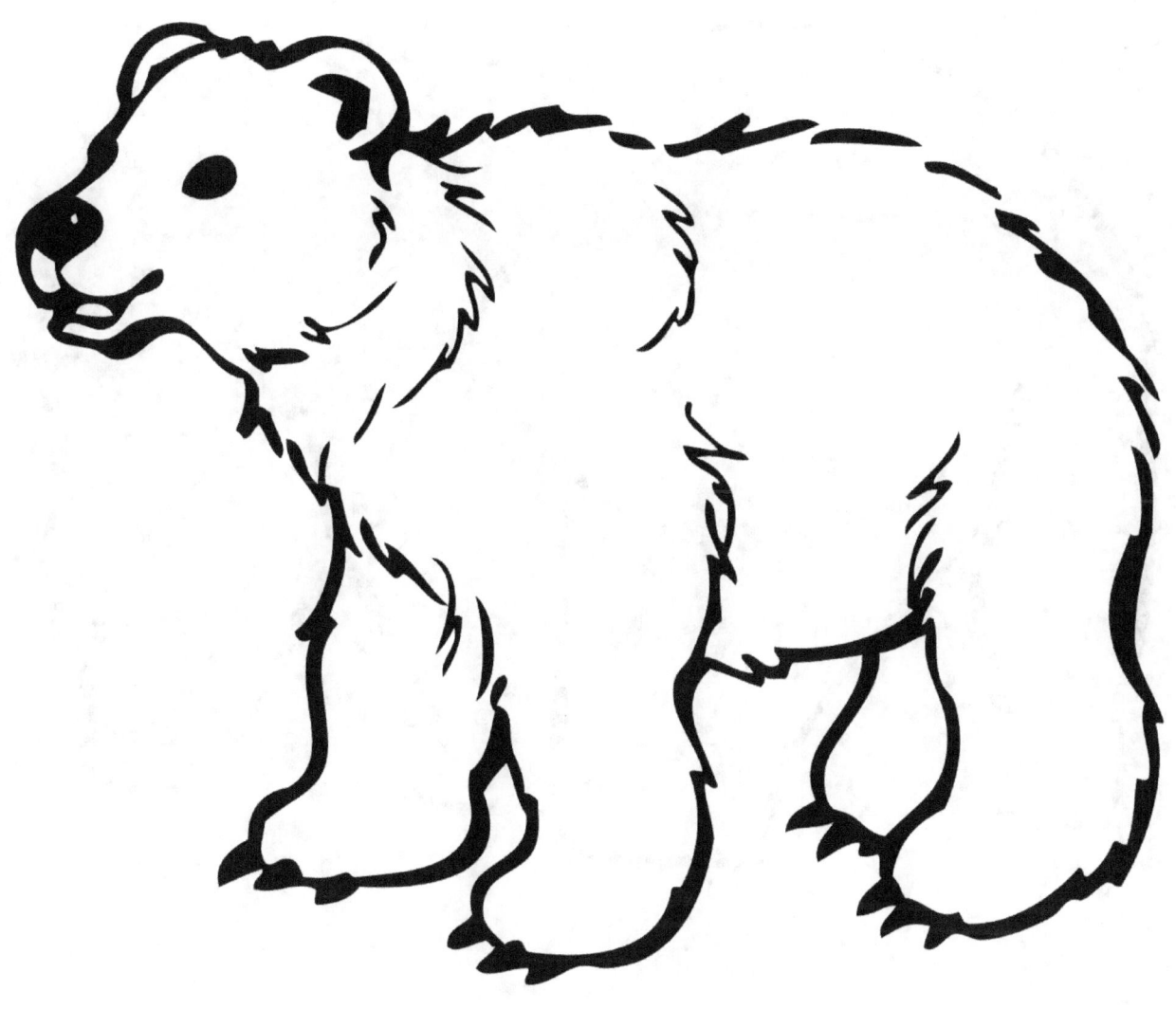

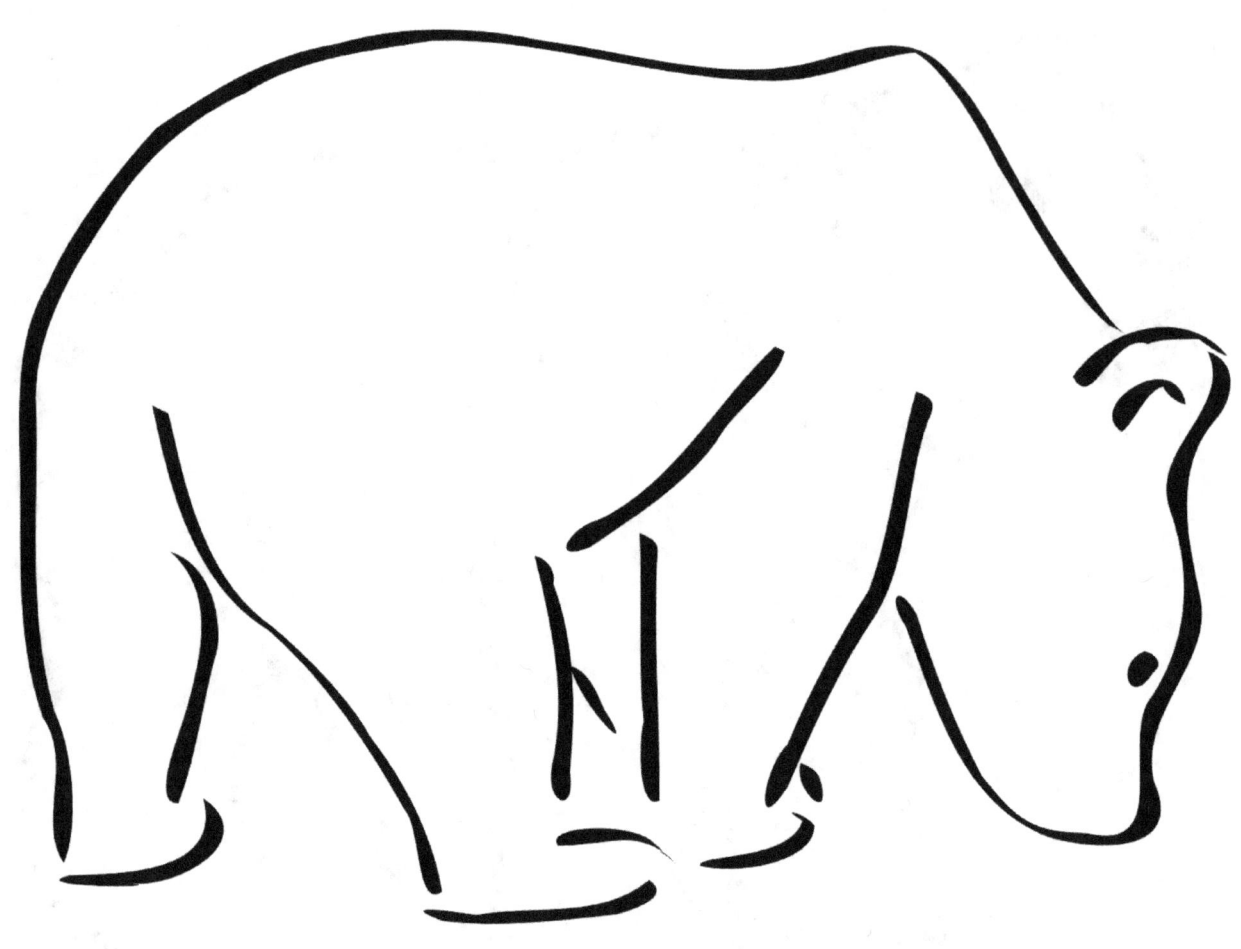

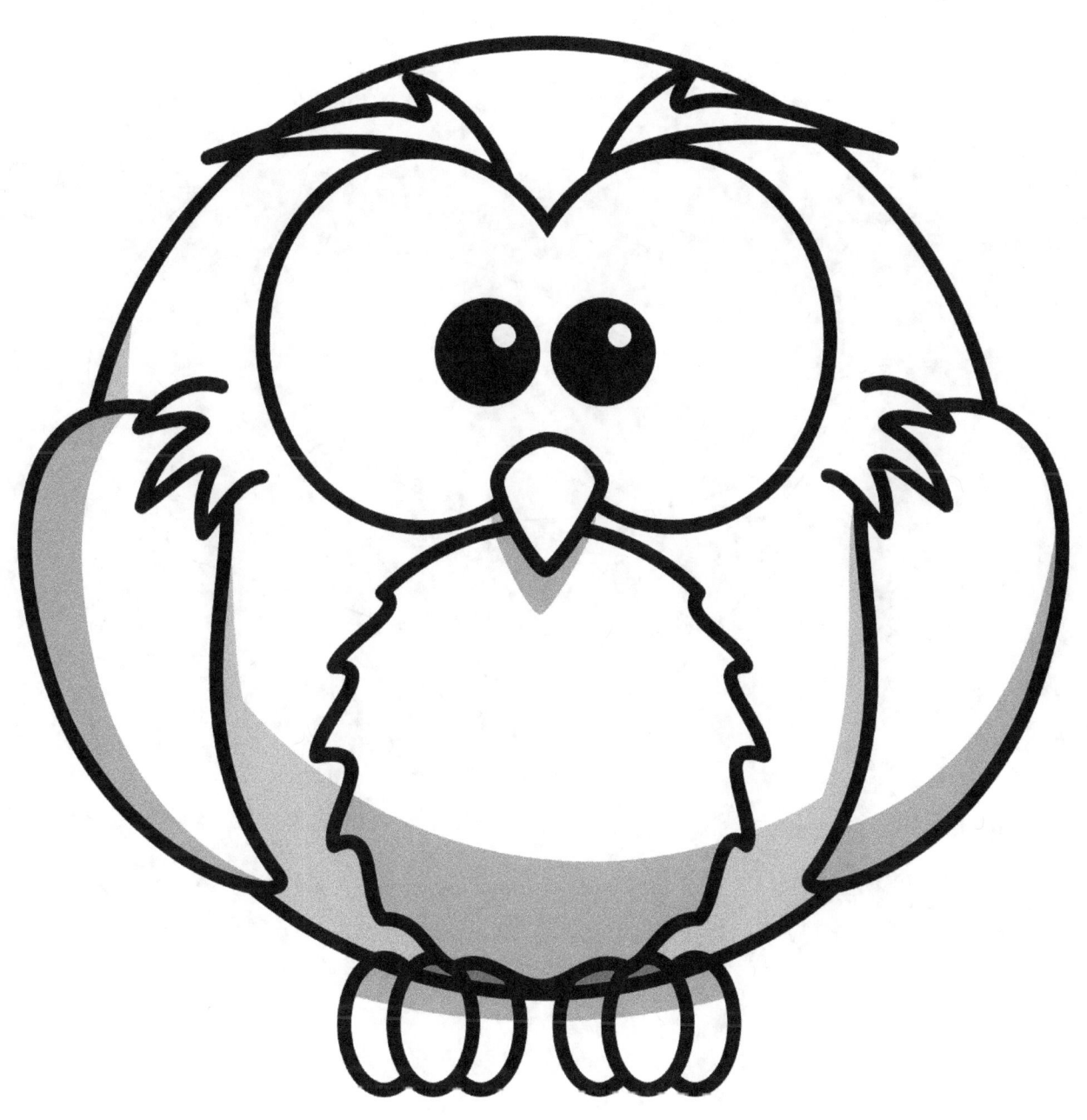

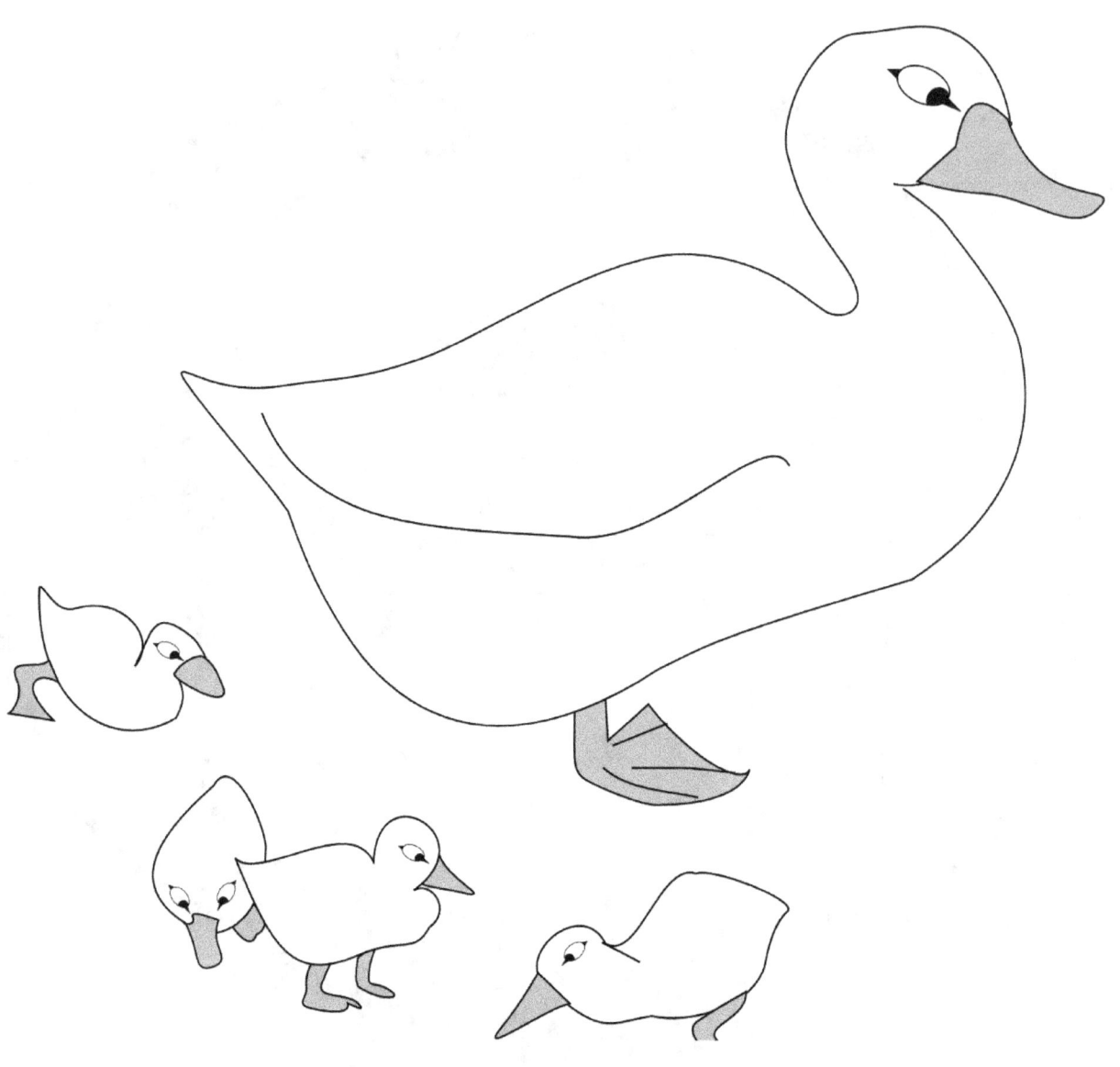

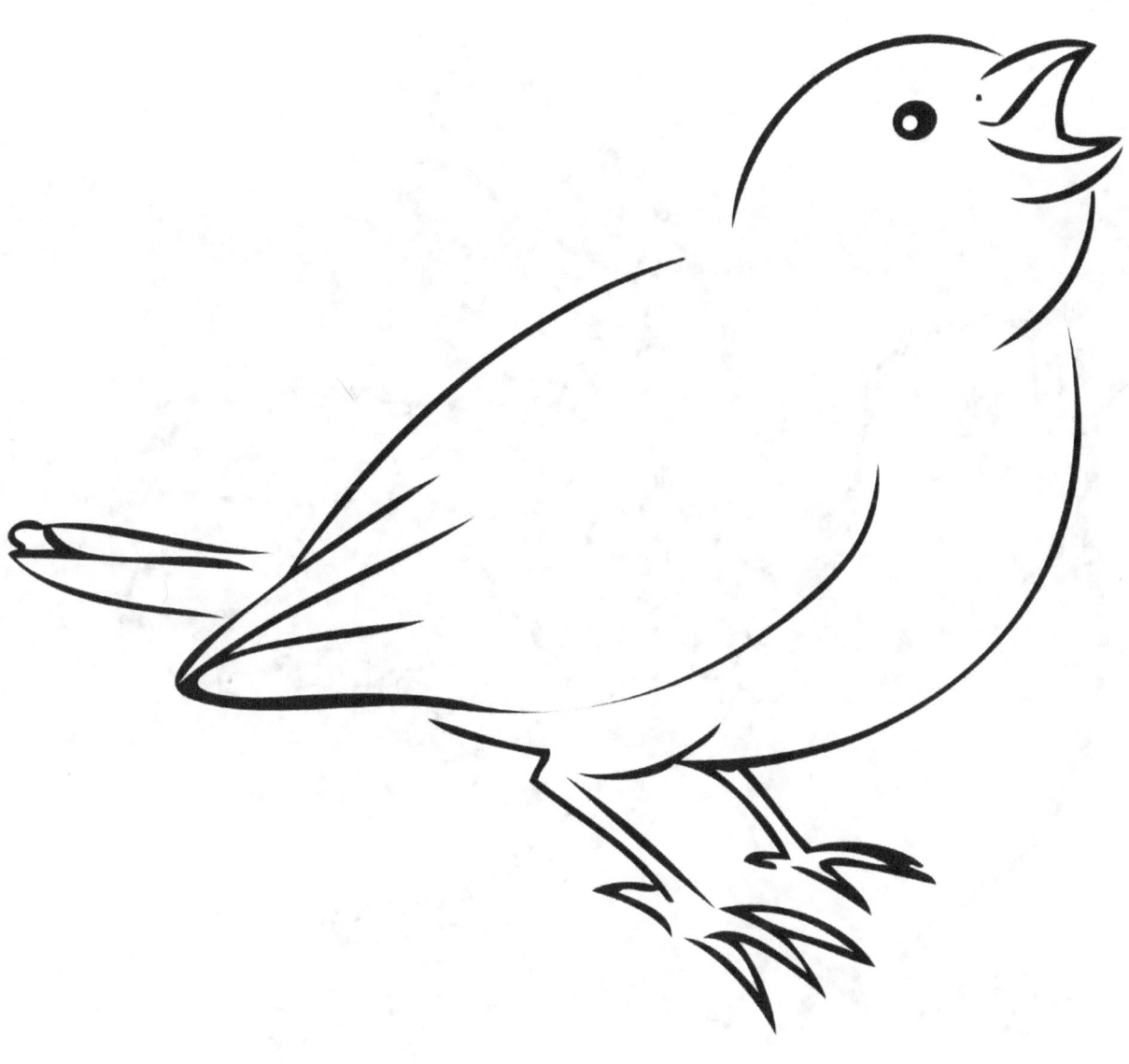

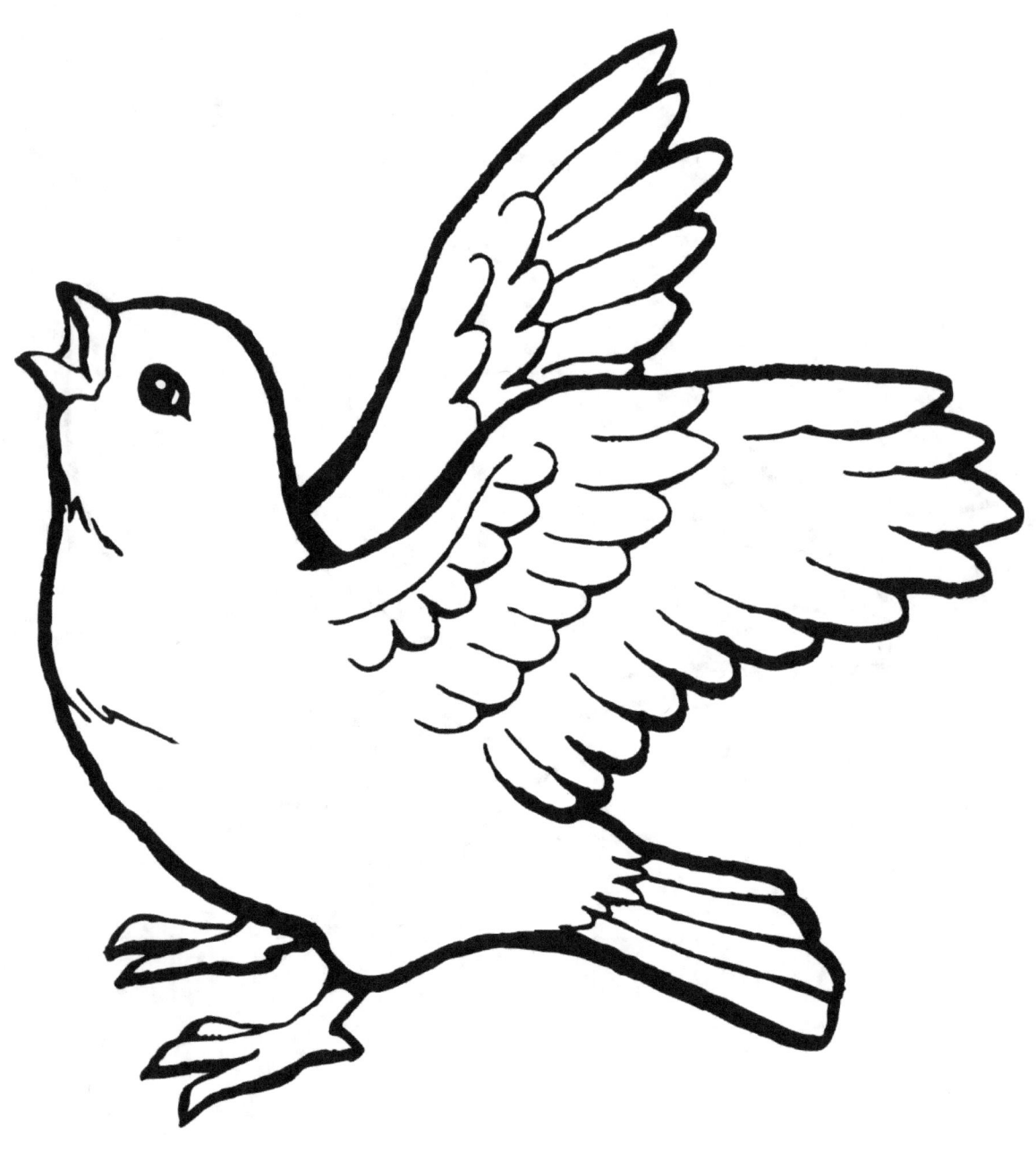

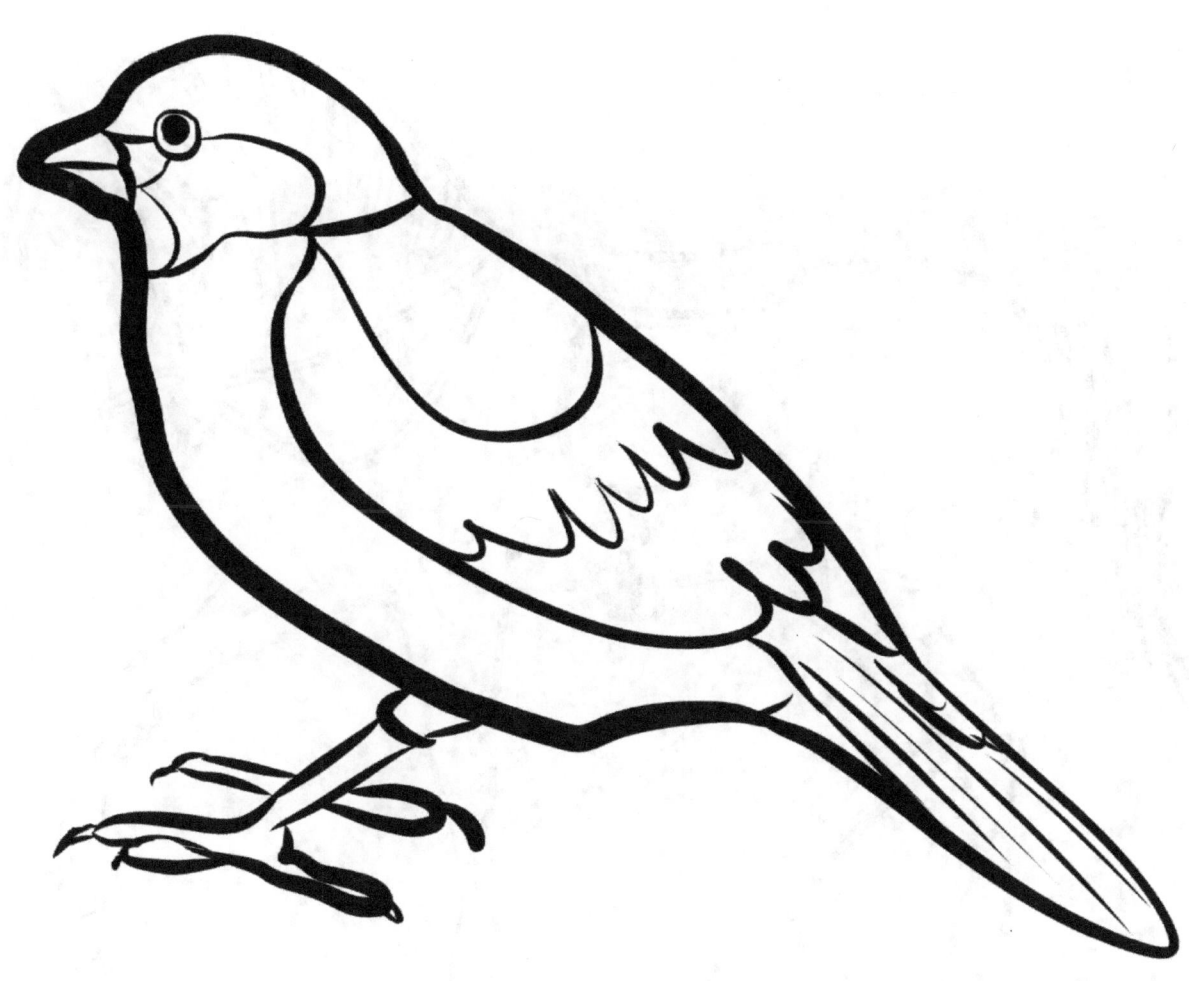

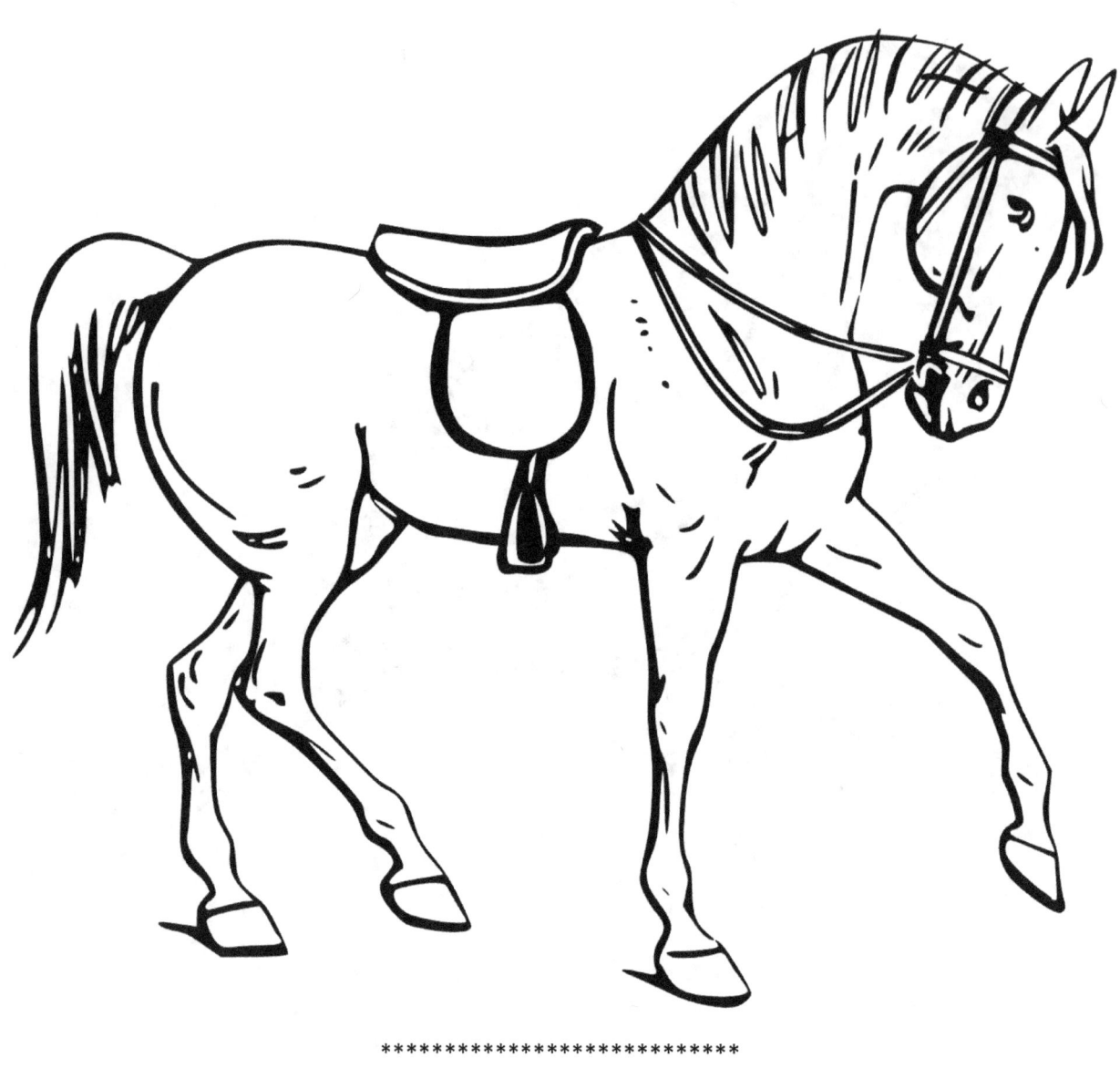

****

www.ingramcontent.com/pod-product-compliance
Lightning Source LLC
Chambersburg PA
CBHW080941220526
45465CB00008BA/3113